SOMEWHERE ELSE

Random Travels on this Small Planet

Merri Melde

The Equestrian Vagabond

For Gramma Turray

CONTENTS

PROLOGUE

I have to go there.

It's a mystery where I got it from, this itch to travel and see new countries, meet different people, and experience unfamiliar cultures. I like to think I inherited a few travel bones handed down by one of my ancestors, maybe one who fled her home country in Eastern Europe, emigrating across an ocean to start a new life in a new country. I was never fleeing anything, though; I just had an urge to get outside my little box and see and experience different places in the world.

For years I was a Budget Backpack Traveler: carrying all my few necessary possessions on my back for months at a time, riding buses and trains and ferries or hitching rides, staying in hostels with other travelers. I had a general itinerary, but it was always quite flexible. Changing plans was sometimes necessary and always a good option to have.

Sometimes it's just about the travel - the freedom to go from here to there on your own, the freedom to wander about. Sometimes it's about the adventure, like a spectacular hike, or a white-water rafting trip. Sometimes it's about the weather or the wildlife or Mother Nature. Sometimes it's about interacting with the locals and getting to know them just a little bit, a visit here, a conversation there. Sometimes it's about the fellow travelers you meet and bond with - backpack travelers are always moving in circuits, sometimes joining up for a while if you're going in the same direction. You often form instant strong friendships, in ways you'd never do with strangers at home. You're more open, since most of you are after the same thing:

exploring and experiencing new places and cultures.

There was a code of conduct that came with backpack traveling. You chose to make your way on your own, not take a guided trip, using a *Let's Go*, or a *Lonely Planet* guidebook for each country, sticking to budget options, and being quite stubborn about it. It was a special way of experiencing a country, though often it was no vacation. You mostly stayed in hostels - *never* a regular hotel, and of course you never *ever* traveled first class on purpose. It was acceptable to use friends' homes as a base, and it was a welcomed respite if you were so lucky.

Someone (possibly Paul Theroux) once said, "Solo travel not only pushes you out of your comfort zone, it also pushes you out of the zone of others' expectations." I never gave a thought to traveling solo. I just wanted to travel, so I did. There's a whole world out there that many of us have the freedom to experience, if we so choose.

As humans, we mostly rely on our senses of sight and hearing to interpret things. Over eons we've lost the heightened perception of smell, but it's an important one tied to our memories.

Every place has a smell that is almost palpable, particularly early mornings. It's almost a seventh sense, one that drills down into your cells, and can be recalled as a distant memory when you go back for a visit. A misty Texas morning smells different than a sagebrush Idaho desert morning, which smells different than a busy New York City sidewalk morning, which smells different than a rural India morning, which smells different than a rainy German village morning, which smells different than a countryside Egyptian morning.

My first overseas travels were easy: six weeks in France, Germany, Switzerland. I specifically went to France just for a horse race, the famed Prix de l'Arc de Triomphe at Longchamp Racecourse in Paris.

Two years later I ambitiously spent three months in Nepal, India, Thailand, and Hong Kong. And the adventures continued over the years, adding up to some 36 countries or thereabouts.

I always met up with people traveling the same circuits. Riding a chair lift up to a castle hostel in Germany, I met South African Janet, whom I later went to visit on a three-month trip in southern Africa. In Nepal I trekked with Norwegian Kjersti, whom I later visited in Oslo, Norway, on a European trip. In Austria I met Amy from Bellingham, Washington (when I lived in Seattle), and months later I ran into her on a hike in the Cascade Mountains in Washington! On a tiny Scottish island I met Tom from Boston, and 30 years later, we are still friends, and living only two states apart now.

Solo backpack travel is not always fun. Sometimes it's hard, scary, disappointing, tiring, challenging. But most of all, it's rewarding. You remember the awful moments well and the brilliant moments best.

I've always kept detailed accounts of my travels, often writing into the wee hours of the nights even when exhausted.

I've spent over two years of my life traveling in other countries, sometimes for pleasure, sometimes for exploration, sometimes for work, but always with the desire to see Somewhere Else.

No matter who you are, you come from Somewhere Else. And Somewhere Else there are people who are different from you, but who are really just like you.

These are some of my stories from my travel journals.

CHAPTER 1: NEPAL, 1991

"It's just over this next hill!"

Why Nepal?

For me, a journey often starts with a photograph. My friend Connie showed me a picture she'd taken during a trek through a high Nepalese village. She and her boyfriend stood beneath colorful prayer flags fluttering in a cold breeze with the snowy Himalaya for a backdrop, and the instant I saw that picture, I thought, *I have to go there.*

Something about a beautiful country with gentle people tucked high away among the mightiest mountains on earth called to me. Even the names - the country of Nepal, and its capital Kathmandu - had an exotic ring to them and conjured up images of something out of *National Geographic.*

And the magical Himalaya - I'd been fascinated by mountain climbing ever since I started to read adventure stories. I wasn't a climber, but I was a hiker. Trekking through the Himalaya mountains was a big thing in Nepal. Just imagine - I could hike to Mount Everest base camp and stand beneath the tallest mountain on earth!

Not much thinking or planning went into my Asian adventure, other than the timeline. The whole trip was rather ambitious: six weeks in Nepal, five weeks in India, followed by a couple of weeks in Thailand and Hong Kong before heading home: three months total on the road.

And so the next year, I boarded a plane for Kathmandu with my backpack and the *Lonely Planet Nepal* and *Trekking the Himalaya* books in hand. Other than vague plans of finding my way to the popular Kathmandu Guest House when I stepped off the plane, and trekking to Mount Everest base camp, I figured I'd work out the rest out when I got there.

I'd never been to a third world country before. In fact, this was only my second backpacker trip. My first one two years earlier was six weeks in France, Germany, Austria, and Switzerland. That was pretty easy.

One of the backpacker's credos (that I instinctively already knew, but that I would live by throughout my worldwide travels) is that you almost always meet the right people and find the right ways to go. If you travel with an open mind, things just fall into place. I just had a vision of standing in a high village beneath colorful fluttering prayer flags, with the Himalaya for a backdrop, and I was on a quest to paint myself in that picture.

And so, I went to Nepal and trekked the Himalaya.

THE HIMALAYA ANNAPURNA CIRCUIT

Thorung La Pass

The air I breathe is sharp and crisp, but stingy with oxygen. I gasp myself awake at nights, craving sleep. Energy comes dear during the daytime. My load is heavy and I struggle to put one foot in front of the other. But there is only one way to go: up.

For eight days we have hiked along narrow trails, from 2,500 feet to 14,600 feet, from jungle to terraced rice fields to forest to alpine tundra to the base of the Himalayan peaks where the Gods rest their toes. We have slogged through deep shadowed canyons and yawning valleys, crossed raging rivers on rickety bamboo bridges, traversed high plateaus, always with snowy peaks of the Himalaya peeking above the horizons, tantalizing us with exotic views, pulling us onward and upward.

From the beginning my pace has matched perfectly that of my trekking partner, Kjersti from Norway. Along the way Andrew from Wales has fallen in with us, and we make a well-paced team, a troika working together to pull our weight and loads up into the mountains of Nepal on the spectacular 180-mile Annapurna Circuit trail.

As we climb higher each day, it becomes more of a trial. My lungs are worn out, my muscles weary, and my joints aching. It's such an effort to strap on my backpack and force my feet to move step by step uphill. So slow... one foot down, next foot down, next foot down. At times I don't dare look up to see how high the daunting trail reaches, just stare at the path and look where my next foot goes. Inexplicably, my pack gains 20 pounds a day. By the end of the long, grueling days, I am certain my trekking partners have slipped rocks in my pack when I'm not looking.

But it is worth the effort. It is hard work, and it is cold, but the sun is bright and the sky an incredible, pure cobalt. And always the mythical and magnetic snow-covered peaks float regally, imperviously above, their gasp-worthy beauty domineering our tiny human endeavors as we edge along their flanks. For good luck, as we pass through villages, we touch the mani walls that ward off spirits that would do us harm, and we turn the prayer wheels (always passing with the wheels on our right, using our clean right hands) for divine fortification on our way up and up. We are not followers of this Buddhist faith, but here, we believe.

Thorung Phedi at 14,895 feet is our final resting place before we conquer Thorung La pass, almost 3,000 feet more above us, the apex of our trek before we reach The Other Side, where life is better, where it's all downhill, and warmer, and our packs are lighter, and oxygen is plentiful.

Our summit day begins at 3 AM when our dorm-mates wake us up far too early. I creep outside to use the toilet, since I'm awake anyway. The stars seem impossibly brilliant, and much larger, in this virginal sky. Surely being 14,000 feet closer to the stars can't make a difference in the size of the stars, but I can almost measure their size between my thumb and forefinger. Perhaps the lack of oxygen, or this early hour is messing with my brain.

Our trio rises at 5 AM, and after breakfast and several steaming cups of coffee, we start our trek at 6:30 as it is getting light. We know it will be a tough day, but we hold a heady optimism and a steady pace, pushing upward, ever higher out of the valley.

After an hour we stop for a water and rest break. We can no longer see the bottom of the valley we left. We still cannot see the tops of the highest peaks above us, because our path rises as a wall in front of us.

After another two hours the hiking truly becomes arduous - false summit after false summit after false summit reaching into thin air. The trail snakes up and up over a ridge - and another solid wall rises above us with the trail shrinking to a ribbon in the distance over the top.

As more of a prayer than confidence, I keep saying, "It's just over this next hill!" The words come spaced apart in gasps. I take three steps and rest. Take three steps and rest. Andrew is behind and below me struggling along. Kjersti is ahead of me, and groans every time the trail shoots out of sight up another false summit.

Our steps get slower and shorter and the breathing more difficult. I no longer look past where my next two feet will go. The views are stunning with every new false summit - but the last part none of us care. All that matters is the next spot I put my foot down, and that I do it without stumbling. Thorung Phedi below us is a distant memory devoured in a bottomless chasm, 2,500 feet below us.

My head begins to hurt, my pack gains weight, my feet feel like anvils dragging through water, and my body refuses to go faster than a crawl. Up here, the air holds half the oxygen it does at sea level. It is laborious to suck in a breath. Now I take two steps and rest, two steps and rest, bending over at the waist to make it easier on my lungs. The hours become a blur. Thorung La pass seems unreachable on this day at this pace, but there is no turning back. My body is running on empty, but the thought of food makes me nauseous and I can't force any more water down.

When, ages later, I dare to lift my eyes beyond my shuffling feet, I spot some rock piles above, and up ahead Kjersti yells, "Ahh haaaa!" - her familiar victory yell - I know the top is truly near. When I see the prayer flags merge into view, I almost collapse with relief.

As our last few steps carry us onto the top, we do practically crumple on the big stone cairn marking Thorung La pass, at 17,769 feet. We're all whooped. And now my altitude headache attacks me full force, but the thrill of being here is not lost on me. Nepal has eight of the world's tallest mountains. Three are within virtual spitting distance: Dhaulagiri, Manaslu, and Annapurna I. A sea of choppy white peaks rises on almost all sides of us. It is a privilege to be up here among them. We are higher than Everest base camp.

But we can't linger. Now ahead of us is The Other Side - oxygen, downhill - but it is more than 5,000 feet down another abyss before we get there. And I am in the throes of Acute Mountain Sickness. I have no drugs with me, so the solution is to descend, as rapidly as possible.

It is miserable. Instead of decreasing, my headache gets worse. I know I am severely dehydrated, but I am incapable of drinking anything. The steep descent is difficult - and therefore not rapid - and often I have to stop and sit a while because I can go no further. After two hours, at another such stop, Andrew takes my big heavy pack (in addition to his) and struggles to carry both down the mountain. I honestly don't know what I'd do without him. I doubt I could make it down. All I want to do is collapse on the trail. I long to just let my legs buckle, and sink to the ground, and never get up again. But I flounder on after Andrew and Kjersti, forcing my legs to keep moving one step down at a time. This isn't exactly how I'd pictured The Other Side.

The next time I stop to sit down, I throw up all my whole day's worth of food and water, which wasn't much in the first place. I feel a bit better then, but still I walk slowly and carefully as it is still very steep, while Andrew blasts way ahead of Kjersti and me with both big backpacks. Kjersti, too, is exhausted, but she keeps plugging along, and I concentrate on following her. Down, and down; we can't even see the bottom of the Kali Gandaki valley we are plunging into.

Finally we spy what must be Muktinath in the far distance, still at least another 1,500 feet down and at least two hours away. *I'm not going to make it,* I think, fighting off queasiness. All I want is a bed and to close my eyes. I don't even need a bed. I can just lay down here and close my eyes. I feel incredibly terrible and weak, when a sudden wave of nausea hits me hard. I barely have time to run off the trail, fall to my knees, and puke my empty insides out.

Andrew throws down our packs and runs uphill to me with Kleenexes and holds my shoulders while Kjersti pulls back my hair and hands me water; and as the spasm racks me and cleans me out, I immediately feel better - so much better that I know now that I am going to make it down on my own two feet.

I am able to keep water down, and we continue down the mountain. I have an easier time walking now, but Andrew is puffing hard a ways behind Kjersti and me. I feel awful that he is still carrying my backpack along with his. But all he says later is, "I'm just glad you walked down on your own! It would have been hell going back up for your pack after helping you down!"

Eventually the slope becomes more reasonable, and soon we pass a large Buddhist temple on the outskirts of Muktinath, a grungy outpost at 12,343 feet, but one of the most beautiful villages I have ever laid eyes on, because I know I have climbed a hell of a mountain and survived this day.

We stumble into the Muktinath Guest House, a rather worn hotel, but one of the most beautiful hotels I have ever been in, because I know I have reached my bed here. Kjersti and I ask for a triple room as Andrew staggers in behind us, unstrapping my big backpack from around his neck before slipping his own pack off.

Still weak, I summon a Herculean effort to lift and carry my own pack upstairs behind the Nepali woman to our room - and I collapse on a bed. This is what I have dreamed of for five hours. I can't move. Andrew digs my sleeping bag out of my pack and throws it over me, and takes off my shoes. I should be embarrassed that Andrew carried my big pack halfway down the mountain, but I simply don't care, and can't do anything but lay there with my head throbbing in pain, wrapped inside my sleeping bag, wearing T-shirt, sweatshirt, wool sweater, and ski jacket, shivering from cold and fatigue.

I wake after an hour. My trekking partners have brought up

a chapati with jam, and fresh mineral water. My severe headache is gone, and I am able to eat and drink, then I sleep more. Later Andrew brings up a cup of milk coffee and props me up in bed. After drinking this and more water, I feel good enough to venture into the downstairs dining room where my tired friends are eating and resting after our 10 straight hours of trekking, 2,874 feet of ascent and 5,426 feet of descent among some of the tallest, most stunning mountain peaks on the planet.

The Nepali woman has placed a bucket of hot coals under the table to warm our legs. I am exhausted, stunned, thrilled - and immensely grateful for this incredible day on top of the world, and the best trekking partners in the world.

She brings us hot cider, garlic soup, and the ubiquitous Nepalese dish of dal bhat.

The Other Side. We have reached The Other Side.

<> <> <> <> <>

note

I did this adventure in 1991. Now, roads are creeping up much of this circuit on both sides - both fortunate and unfortunate for businesses along the trekking route, and decidedly unfortunate for trekking purists. But roads will never make it all the way around the Annapurna circuit. Nothing will take away from the magnificence of trekking the high trails in the Himalaya, and the monumental accomplishment of conquering the paths on your own two feet.

CHAPTER 2:
INDIA, 1991

"Chaotic cacophony"

India was never on my Bucket List. I had no spiritual aspirations, no urge to visit yogis or hang out with sadhus. In fact, why on earth did I want to go to India anyway? I don't like being around crowds of people. India had approximately 1,429,004,385 people at any one time. (I must have run into half of them.) I mostly went to India because it was right below Nepal where I definitely wanted to go, and, since I had Indian friends to visit in Madras (now Chennai), in the south of the country, I would just head south from Nepal.

It was quite a shock going from Nepal, where, in general, everything was laid back and easy to figure out and the people were gentle and quiet and polite, to India where, in general, everything wasn't and many people weren't. Some places in India were desperately poor and the people worked desperately harder to earn a rupee. So many times their desperation was a physical and confounding jolt to my system.

I like to anonymously blend in with people; in India as a blond white female I stuck out like a sore thumb. I don't like to be hassled; I like to keep a low profile. I would find none of this in India.

Basically, I went to India because of its location below Nepal, my primary destination, and because my Indian friends had invited me to visit. (It would turn out that my friends were out of the country in Sri Lanka, so after I adventurously made my way to the south of India, I eventually joined them in Sri Lanka.)

In fact when I planned my six weeks in Nepal, I didn't really have concrete plans for the following five weeks in India, other than starting in Delhi in the north, and visiting the Taj Mahal, and making it to Madras at the bottom of the country. How hard could it be?

I had no idea that India was an extreme bombardment of the senses: overwhelming sights, sounds, smells, all at high volume, all the time. The country was a study in extremes: a few exceptional highs and many vexing lows. It's one of the worst places I've ever traveled and one of the most incredible places I've ever traveled.

I had no idea merely getting from one place to another, and indeed even staying in one place, would be so exhausting, so frustrating, so maddening, so brilliant, so intense. I would learn that when I wanted anything - a ride, a place to stay, food, a drink of purified water - I would have to incessantly bargain. I did not yet understand that when you have to pee, you will have to hold it (if you're a woman). I would discover that I would never be far from the madding crowd; I would always be in the midst of it.

Keep in mind that these travels were before cell phones and internet (if you can imagine such a world). You might find pay phones from which to call, if they worked, or, if you could find a fax machine, if it worked you could send and receive faxes, if someone at the other end had a fax machine.

The *Lonely Planet* books were the current Bibles for travelers; hopefully, since the books came out at least a year after they were written, listed hotels were still in existence and their phone numbers were still working - if you could find a pay phone, if it worked, and if it was the right number and if anybody answered at the other end. We often relied on the *Lonely Planet* for places to stay and places to eat and how to get from one place to another. And if the book was outdated, and the hotels or train stations weren't there anymore, well, gird your loins and good luck to you.

Sometimes it was hard to have a sense of humor, but at other times, that infinitesimal twinkle of hilarity in the insanity was what got me through to the next place in India.

India was so much harder to travel in as a backpacker - particularly as a blond female - so exhausting, so wearing, that most backpackers lost weight traveling in India. I myself cannot gain weight to save my life. However, for the first time in my life, I gained weight while traveling in India. I ate everything and I loved everything I ate, and I ate more of it. I often never knew what I was ordering; I just pointed at names on a menu. I loved every bite, of everything. The act of eating Indian food was one thing that always gave me moments of comfort, no matter how crazy the maelstrom around me. I gained so much weight I mailed my jeans home because I could no longer fit in them (and mailing the box was an adventure in itself that only India could provide).

Looking back, with time and space - decades of space - I can say I'm glad I traveled in India, and it was quite the adventure. But I still don't want to go back.

And so, I went to India, and I bring you some adventures from this profoundly exasperating, amazing country.

DELHI

December 2

I'd met German Anneli during my last days in Kathmandu, Nepal, and since we were both coincidentally (and very conveniently) flying to Delhi on the same day, we'd decided to hook up and travel together through India.

Thank goodness. It was a lucky decision, as I found out quickly that even with a travel partner, things for backpack travelers are not easy in India, particularly as a blond non-Indian female traveler.

Anneli and I planned to meet by the bank in the Delhi airport. She was supposed to land an hour after I did. I didn't want to think about what might happen if she didn't... so I just didn't think about it.

I would be relying on my Travel Bible - the *Lonely Planet India* - but I sure hoped Anneli and I would hook up or I'd have to figure everything out on my own.

I was a bit jazzed, after my 90-minute flight, when I landed in Delhi. Wow! I'm in India! I made it through customs with a minimum of hassle, changed money (25.5 rupees to the dollar, that was a good rate), efficiently retrieved my backpack from baggage claim, and sat there trying to wait patiently for Anneli to show up. All the same, I pulled out my *Lonely Planet* and tried to figure how I was going to get to Paharganj, where we'd decided to stay in a hotel, on my own if worst came to worst and she didn't arrive. (This was, of course, before cell phones, so there was no way to contact her.)

Weeks ago, Anneli had spent one night in Delhi flying to

Kathmandu, so she already knew how to get around, and I was appalled at how much I already was already depending on her to show up.

And, finally, there she was! After expecting to hook up with her, it was such a relief to actually do it. She knew what bus to get on leaving the airport and how much it cost.

I'd been on crowded buses before, but this one took the cake. I felt like a sardine squished in a can with a hundred other fishies. I got a seat, but not much of one because I had to share it with a woman *and* my big pack, and my pack had the most room. We both had one butt cheek on the same seat. I was wedged where I could not move. People were stuffed in the aisles and kept falling over each other and their bags, so I guess I was lucky.

We spilled off the bus at the New Delhi railway station, looking for Main Bazaar road, and were immediately swarmed by dozens of people: "Hello madam – taxi? Rickshaw? Scuze me? Where are you going Hotel? Very good rooms madam two rupees no more Hello..." It wasn't too hard to say no and tune them out and keep moving forward, but, wow, what an assault on the senses after the tranquility of Nepal.

By looking at my handy compass, I realized we were on the east side of the station and we needed the west side. We waded through crowds around the building, and found Main Bazaar road with no problem, though we were still hounded by rickshaw and little taxi drivers offering us the greatest ride deals.

It was good practice ignoring them, as I'd continue to be in this situation all over India for the next five weeks. A few times beggars brushed my leg as I passed by, but I disregarded them also. We would quickly learn you had to steel yourself to many things in India, turn off your empathy meter and keep going, because the desperate people with desperate problems were overwhelming in numbers and desperation, and nothing you did could help them. Giving one a few rupees was not going to chance a single aspect of his or her life, and would only create demands, from him and suddenly dozens of others, demanding more help. It would be gut-wrenching if you let it get to you, and there was *so much* of it.

After walking a few blocks, we found, with no problem, the Hotel Navrang we'd picked out for a few nights. We got a room with a "bath," here in India meaning a toilet, with no shower or actual bath, for 70 rupees. It looked shabby, but this is India, and Nepal had looked shabby at first. India was just Different. (This would become an all-purpose word!)

The man led us up several flights of stairs (they had no elevator, of course) to our room with a fan. Thank goodness we had a fan, because it would have been warm and stuffy without.

Of course I was starving and thirsty, so we waded back out into the Delhi traffic and humanity and picked the Maadan Café for sustenance. We sat amongst plenty people and lots of flies, but, looking on the positive side, at least they weren't obnoxious flies.

The man handed us menus and pointed to the "Southern Indian" dishes, even though we were in Northern India. I hadn't heard of any of them, but we ordered all of it, and boy was it good! The food was cheap, and I had a feeling I was going to be eating a *lot* of Indian food and I would love all of it.

After dinner, following a map in our book, we walked, still continuously hounded by rickshaw drivers, toward the Lakshmi Narayan Temple. At one point we cut down a road through what looked to be a high-rise housing project, and a few things flew down at us: two Tihar necklaces and a small rock. Is that the Indian way of saying Welcome to our Neighborhood?

The temple was open only to Hindus, and I agreed with the *Lonely Planet*'s description: a modern garish temple. I didn't pretend to understand anything about Hinduism other than it being the third largest religion in the world after Christianity and Islam. From an outsider glancing in, there were too many gods with unfamiliar names to remember, and there was a lot of festive color.

The Main Bazaar road we walked back on was now a massive jam of peoplescootercyclerickshawsbikes, and a few cows here and there, ignoring the chaos. I should learn the zen of being a cow in India. These Brahmans were not mean like ours in the U.S., although I was almost impaled on a Brahman's head. It wasn't his horns because this one had no horns, but I wasn't looking ahead where I was walking, I was looking backwards, something you don't do here in India, and I turned to see a cow's head just about in my belly, and I danced out of the way just in time.

While strolling and dodging traffic and people along the way, some Indian kids ran alongside us, giggling, and asked me for my autograph. They thought it was funny, and they wouldn't say why, so I scribbled something totally illegible on their notebook paper. They cackled some more, and kept following us, and then finally got up their nerve to ask Anneli for her autograph. "No no, sorry," she snorted, striding along, and the kids giggled anyway and ran off.

We walked and walked, but I was ready to go back and fall into bed in the hotel. My eye was scratchy, my throat was sore and killing me, and I was tired from a lingering cold. Anneli had a cold too. It must be the Indian dust and exhaust that was making us worse, after the clean mountain air of Nepal.

Our "bath" had only cold water and it was too cool even to sponge off. I was disappointed with the bed; it had only one sheet over the mattress, with nothing for cover, so I slept in sweats and used the sleepsheet I brought with me, and scrunched up a sweatshirt for a pillow.

< > < > < > < > < >

December 3

I felt like hell when I woke up, with my head so clogged I could hardly breathe. Half of that goes away with coffee though, and we went out to another café. I wanted fruit curd; the waiter said no. So I ordered a cheese omelet, which of course they forgot, but at least I was served toast with jam and butter, and

18

after plenty of good coffee, I felt better and ready to tackle Delhi.

After breakfast, we decided to go to Connaught Place, one of the main commercial, financial, and business centers in New Delhi, so that Anneli could find a bus to the Thai embassy. I wanted a travel agent to see about a bus or train for us to Agra, and I wanted directions to the New Delhi General Post Office, hoping I would have mail waiting there for me.

We found the Delhi Transport Corp, which was supposed to have bus schedules and routes, which they did, but it was all in Hindi and of no use to us.

Then Anneli decided to take an autorickshaw to the embassy. The first guy wanted 60 rupees (about two dollars - outrageous!) but she said no. So we walked onward, dogged incessantly with hassle hassle hassle from every shop or stall that we passed. "Scuze me, madam? Change money, shawl? Best quality! Come look. That's OK you don't have to buy just look. Nice shawl for you best quality good price you can look this way." I also ignored a guy following me and shoving Fine Quality Postcards in my face.

These guys didn't stop! Shawls, postcards, chess sets, a paper for me to sign (I guess to donate money), rickshaw, taxi, where are you going, beggars begging Anneli and me the white people (but not any Indians) walking by, daring us to look at their deformities and pay money, sellers dangling their Best Quality wares. I was good at putting on my expressionless face and tuning out the noise, so I wasn't so bothered today, but I supposed in a week I would be!

We split up; Anneli went a different direction toward her embassy, and I passed the tempting United Coffee House, which looked too nice and pricey for the likes of me, the Grubby Budget Traveler. Instead I found and slipped into the Don't Pass Me By restaurant, down an alley, recommended in the *Lonely Planet*. I sat down at the only empty back table, miraculously not being bothered, only waited on by a pleasant waiter, enjoying the rare peace for a while. I scarfed two miniature orange cool sodas and a large plate of veggie fried rice for less than a dollar.

My stomach satisfied temporarily, I walked back to Wenger's, the famous dessert place, where Anneli was waiting. We dove into some delicious pastries, which we deserved for all the work we were putting into roaming through Delhi!

Of course, when you're in India, you must shop, no matter the hassles, because Indian garments can be so beautiful. We visited the crowded, loud, cramped, hot zoo of Palika Bazaar, a famous underground market near Connaught Place, where Anneli looked at Indian outfits known as a shalwar kameez and churidar - the baggy pants covered by a long knee-length shirt and scarf.

The jolly man pulled outfits out of packages, and if Anneli said no, "No!" he said, and tossed it aside as rubbish. If she said "Yes, that's pretty," he had it wrapped and in a bag before she could blink.

I asked if one outfit she was considering came with a scarf. "Yes we cut you one," the man said with a flourish, and snapped his fingers, and one of his helpers started to cut one from cloth until I yelled, "No No! Wait! Don't cut it yet, she doesn't want this one!"

"Oh!" the man said, and tossed it away on the rubbish pile, "No good! *This* is for you. Very, very nice. Good color on you. You like? Good!", and it was wrapped and shoved in a bag and handed to me, and I was not even shopping!

This delightful and hilarious encounter was such a welcomed respite from the constant hassles. We all enjoyed it, particularly the man who owned the shop. He had stuffed three different outfits in a bag, with Anneli's backpack plopped on top and shoved into my hands before Anneli could say no.

She ultimately decided on a black and gold suit, with the black scarf, for 320 rupees (roughly $12). She looked smashing in it. We left there laughing. Anneli said she wouldn't have even looked for an outfit by herself. It's always more fun to shop in company.

It was already dark, so we walked back to the Main Bazaar area in Paharganj, stopping at the New Delhi train station to see about the train to Agra.

What another zoo! There were more people in there than rush hour at Penn Station in New York City! We had no clue what counter to go to; we did find the tourist information place upstairs but it had closed.

Dinner was at a different restaurant where I ordered some Indian dish I'd never heard of. This veggie-something with a sort of fried potato in a curry of hot gravy, with a cheese nan and butter paratha (flatbread), was delicious.

On the way back to our hotel we encountered a band, playing badly off key for a wedding. In fact I think they were all playing different songs. A bejeweled and cloaked white horse stood by. From having read the book *City of Joy*, I knew a groom was supposed to arrive on a white horse. The horse was there, but the groom had yet to make an appearance. We didn't stick around to see what happened, because there was a human traffic jam, and the band merrily playing all their 30 different songs at once was deafening.

On our way up to our room tonight, we finally officially signed in to the hotel when the counter man waved us down. As he copied information from my passport, he asked how I found this hotel, had I been to Delhi before?

I explained about my U.S. friends Connie and Lawrence, who had visited a few years earlier, and showed him a picture, and, oh yes! He remembered both of them.

< > < > < > < > < >

December 4

Delhi today was exhausting, interesting, hectic, an exasperating hassle.

First, breakfast: milk coffee, banana curd, and I asked for some kind of Indian bread with jam, and instead got some sort of potato pancake with peas in it. It was delicious, though. Good thing I like everything here so far, because I never know what

I'm ordering, and I never know if I'll get what I order.

We were headed for Old Delhi: the Jama Masjid, Red Fort, General Post Office, and Chandni Chowk, one of Old Delhi's oldest and busiest markets.

Delhi wasn't quite so crowded this morning. We asked at the train station tourist information office about a train to Agra: do we need to make a reservation to travel there second class? The lady said no, just show up before the train leaves. We wrote down a few times and trains to choose from later on.

I was already looking for a toilet, but didn't see one anywhere here, though surely the railway station had toilets. I would discover, unfortunately and uncomfortably, that finding toilets for women is sometimes impossible in India.

We walked on (hounded by rickshaw drivers) to the Jama Masjid, a mosque built in 1644-1656 AD by the same Mughal emperor Shah Jahan who built the Taj Mahal (which we would see in Agra), and still Delhi's primary mosque. The mosque is crowded Fridays for prayer, and it is packed solid during the Eid al-Fitr festival, the "Breaking of the Fast" of Ramadan.

Here were the Delhi throngs, even though it was only Wednesday. It was crowded and crazy walking there, elbow to elbow human traffic meeting elbow to elbow human traffic with the occasional strolling cow in the mix.

From the outside, the mosque was quite a majestic building. We walked around to the south entrance and up the steps, where we had to pay five rupees each and take our shoes off. It wasn't *too* dirty in there, although pigeons have left their marks in many places and I found one of those marks with one of my socks.

The mosque is one of the largest in India, with a capacity of 25,000. The alternating red sandstone and white marble dazzles, especially when you think how long ago this was built – way before they had cranes and bulldozers and glue guns and Makitas.

Not two minutes after we walked in, three little boys swarmed us. One did the talking. "Hello one rupee."

I said, "Hello give me five rupees?" and held out my hand. That was a shocking novelty to him – he got a puzzled look, shook his head, then grinned.

"Hello one rupee."

I responded, "Hello give me five rupees?"

They withdrew laughing, and followed us around the mosque the entire time, occasionally coming up to try again for one rupee. I either ignored them, or kept asking for five rupees.

Another group of kids came up. One older boy wanted to shake my hand, so I did, and he said "One rupee?"

I said "Hello give me give five rupees?" He was so confused he and his group withdrew.

I'd learned in Nepal that if, with good, friendly intentions, you hand out a few coins or a few trinkets to three kids, suddenly 30 appear around you demanding their handouts, and parents also appear and are none too happy with you.

Around noon, the mosque closed to non-Muslims, and Muslims were beginning to spread out several lines of carpets to kneel on and pray. The mosque faces west, towards Mecca.

We drifted out to put our shoes on, one little boy still expecting a rupee, jumping up every time I opened my pack for my camera or book.

Back into the Hassle and Bustle of Old Delhi, we plowed our way towards the Red Fort. Passing through a row of trinket stalls around the front of the mosque, we walked away from the main entrance, stared at, hissed at, approached by a mendicant I danced around, begged by an armless leper entrenched where we had to step around him.

We could plainly see the Red Fort ahead, but we had to walk north to get to the main entrance, and then try to cross the street, with a massive amount of cars and trucks and tuk-tuks and bicycles and motorcycles and humans and always a cow or two, going both directions, which was more dangerous than trying to run across the track in front of the start of the Kentucky Derby. Crossing some of the streets here is a death wish. Finally we made it in one piece across the road to the safety of the sidewalk, though I almost lost a foot to a car on the way.

There was a carnival/circus in front of the ancient fort. Two little Indian girls surged up to us and held out their hands for money, and even my brushing them off wouldn't deter them. I'd rub them off in a wave of oncoming people, and one would pop right up again, holding out her hand and poking or brushing my leg.

Anneli and I had to stand and wait on traffic on a side street, the girls still crowding us, and when we crossed the street, dodging cars and motorcycles, we lost them. I didn't even look back to see if they tried to follow us across.

Were these two little girls homeless? Begging money for their family? Begging money for their boss or pimp? Were they beaten if they didn't bring money back? Would they starve to death? You just couldn't go down these rabbit hole thoughts with the staggering number of beggars and poor people everywhere.

The Red Fort is another impressive work of architectural art, not only for its striking color, with lots of contrasting white marble buildings inside, but for its size: the walls extend almost a mile and a half, and range in height from 60 to 100 feet. How did these people build like this, way back then?

That favorite fifth Mughal King of ours, Shah Jahan, built this fort from 1638-1648, starting construction after the Taj Mahal was begun. He never completely moved his capital from Agra to Shahjahanabad (the walled city of Old Delhi) because his son Aurangzeb, the sixth and last Mughal, got tired of his pop's architectural extravagances (or, perhaps it was more about power struggles), and imprisoned him in his own Red Fort until he died.

We entered the Red Fort through the Lahore Gate. It took its name from Lahore in Pakistan, where the gate faces, which is where the fourth Mughal King is buried.

From the inside, the fort's size is so immense you can't see the walls. It could house an entire city. Part of it is now a military ground. It was easy to imagine the courtyard full of horses and important people moving about.

But back to reality, it was full of staring Indians and a few jerks, a group of a half-dozen older boys who hassled me and tried to corner me and said some things to me; even in Hindi it was obviously not nice, and I was getting pissed. Finally I lingered too long in one place and they moved on. There were too many other people around so I wasn't worried, but I was uncomfortable. Anneli was getting similarly harassed.

We strolled through Halls for Public Audiences and Private Audiences, and royal baths, and a marble mini-mosque. Outside, 30 feet below the walls, east of the fort were a few beggars performing tricks for money – a magician who 'flew,' a snake charmer, all of whom demanded money, but they couldn't climb up the walls to get it, so they were often out of luck, I bet. This same scene probably played out 400 years ago, with beggars, performers, and common people outside the walls performing or asking or begging for money.

By now I had to pee so bad I was seeing cross-eyed, but there was no toilet anywhere. All over the city, on the sidewalks, on busy streets, are stalls or walls, with or without a wall as screen, for men to pee. But *nothing* for women. What - so women don't get to pee? It's discrimination! It's irritating that men can whip it out anytime and anywhere – and they do here, whether it's a toilet or not, whether it's out in the open or not - and we women have to suffer! Men just pee on walls on the busy sidewalks and you just walk on around them and are expected to avert your gaze. And apparently women just must hold it.

We had to stop at the Old Delhi GPO next, to check for letters. This was long before the internet and emails made life easy, so
I used this GPO address for receiving forwarded mail. Getting actual mail while on the road was so exciting! It wasn't a long walk, but crossing the streets, and slowly weaving through standstill traffic, was a trial.

Several times in Delhi, like today, I'd been purposely bumped into by oncoming people, which really irritated me, but

I made sure they got as hard a blow as I did. I felt like a hockey player sometimes. Nepalis did all they could to avoid bumping into you.

All that work getting to the post office was for nought; disappointingly, I had no letters waiting for me.

And of course there was no bathroom around here either, and my bladder was starting to have conniption fits. I thought the best chance for a toilet might be a restaurant, and so we walked on to the Chandni Chowk market to look for any of the restaurants recommended in the *Lonely Planet.* What another zoo!

There were so many little shops crammed together, and people jammed together. In some places we had to shove our way through walls of people. We saw only a few food stalls with booths, all occupied; the other few were stand-and-eat-and-go. Anneli tried asking at a few restaurants for a toilet, but she only drew a crowd of nodding, staring Indians. She tried a man in a shop who agreeably nodded and pointed to an Indian food stall, where the restaurant man nodded at us. There were no bathrooms.

I finally said, "I've gotta go back to the hotel to pee!" We tried a cycle rickshaw for a ride back.

I let Anneli do the talking because I *hated* to do it. She asked one guy, "Main Bazaar? Paharganj? How much? Two rupees?" She held up two fingers.

OK, he nodded, seeming to agree on two rupees. We climbed in, and he pulled over twice, once at a little police post, and we figured he was asking them for directions.

Our guy pedaled along, bumped along, avoided other wheeled vehicles, and at one place where we sat motionless in traffic, a guy walked by and reached in our rickshaw and squeezed my bicep. I think he was reaching for my boob but missed. Argh!

I marveled at the muscle strength these cyclers have. The cycle rickshaw in front of us had *five* people in it. Our guy found his way to the east side of the railway station, then started over the bridge over the railroad trains, having to get off and pull us along the uphill part.

I thought we'd be nice and get off at the stairs at the other side of the tracks, and we'd just walk down to the Main Bazaar, so I pointed to the steps and the curb. He stopped, we got out, and Anneli handed him two rupees.

He wouldn't take it, and started talking to three uniformed guys (not cops, just "officers, watching the world go by," said Anneli). Possibly he was complaining to them how far he brought us and we weren't paying him enough.

Anneli forced the two rupee note in his hand, and I gave him another two, but he refused it. I said, "You said two rupees. She gave you two rupees, I'm giving you two more, that's four rupees. Do you want it, or not?"

He put his hand down and wouldn't take it; the three not-cops seemed amused, and several more Indians had stopped to stare, so Anneli and I shrugged and started walking off with our money he had refused.

We started down the steps, and we heard "Hey! Hello!" The guy was leaning over the rail, looking down at me. I said, exasperated, "Do you want this or not?!" and I handed it up to him. "Then take it!" I shoved it in his hand and walked on.

I am sure it was a miscommunication. The two fingers Anneli held up for us meant two rupees, and for him it probably meant two passengers. But I was so irritated, everything was such a hassle, and ohmigod I had to pee so badly and there was no place to pee for women in this city!

We finally made it back to our room, where I peed for 10 minutes, or so it seemed.

Then, refreshed and ready to hit it again, we were hungry! We picked a new place where Anneli had a quick sandwich and then left for the Thai embassy. I stayed and ate the veggie biryani, which turned out to be a big plate of spicy rice with a raw slice of onion, tomatoes and cucumber. I didn't think that was really biryani, but it again was delicious.

As I sat there, finishing my drink and writing and

enjoying the brief respite from the draining madness of Delhi, suddenly I got thumped on the head. I looked up, startled, into a white hippy's smiling face. "10 rupees."

Baffled, I said, "Excuse me?"

He repeated, smiling beatifically, "10 rupees."

I managed to reply, "No, sorry," and he walked out smiling, and I thought – did that really happen? Why didn't he thump anybody else on the head? Do these things only happen to me? I'd seen a lot of people who looked like they left the 1960s San Francisco hippy scene to live here in Delhi cheaply and happily. Even the people in our guest house are different. It's not the usual travel scene, at least here in Delhi, that it is in Europe, or Nepal.

I met Anneli outside our hotel, and as she stood and looking in her *Lonely Planet* book, and I stood beside her looking over her shoulder, some asshole in a group of guys passing me poked me in the butt! Naturally I jumped, but by the time they turned back to look at me and laugh, I was standing there still looking at Anneli's book with her, my expression unchanged, pretending I hadn't experienced that.

I was torn between being angry and cracking up - should I run after and scream at them or collapse in hysterics?

After another good dinner at another restaurant, we were both worn out from our Delhi adventures today. We stayed up until after 12:30 talking, which was good thing, because people in this hotel were so noisy. Music, blabbing, yelling, slamming doors...

< > < > < > < > < >

December 5

Get me out of Delhi! What a crazy madhouse! I'm never coming back if all of India is like this. That was the opening line in my journal for December 5 and the theme of the entire day.

I felt awful again when I woke up, as if I'd gotten three

hours of sleep. Maybe I did.

We went to breakfast and I ordered milk coffee, toast and jam, and fruit curd. The coffee and toast came, but no fruit curd.

After an extra stop at our hotel for the toilet one more time, because we knew we wouldn't find any toilets out there in the city for women, we walked to the post office, hounded by rickshaw drivers the entire way, "Hello madam, post office?" Even when we were a block away, a few of them hadn't given up.

Anneli mailed a letter, and I bought postcard stamps, with a minimum of fuss.

Our goal for the rest of the day was to get to Qutab Minar, an ancient minaret (and, in 1993, it would become a UNESCO World Heritage Site), via bus 505 in front of the DTC (Delhi Transport Corporation) in Connaught Place, or on another bus mentioned in Anneli's German *Lonely Planet* book.

Many buses zoomed by, but only one or two slowed down, without stopping, to spit off a few passengers, and they hit the ground running. All destinations were written on the top of the buses in Hindi, which we couldn't decipher. Some buses had numbers, some didn't.

Anneli was only able to ask one driver if he was headed to Qutab Minar, and he sped off even as he was shaking his head. We waited about an hour, in the meanwhile asking a DTC guy if we could get on the evening tour at Qutab Minar, but he said, "No, not possible. Full," but he really just wanted to keep yapping with his buddy instead of sell any tickets.

He did point us to the government tourist office across the street. We literally waited for ten minutes to try crossing this street, and finally gave up and walked down to the corner to use the subway, the underground crosswalks.

The tourist office person said tours were unavailable, so we decided to go stand at a different place, by the Super Bazaar, which was at least a designated bus stop. None of the four different stops listed the 505 bus, but we stood near the two stops that had other #500 buses. We waited, and waited.

Anneli started asking some bus drivers that stopped if

they were going to Qutab Minar, and she either got a reply of a head shake, or a puff of black exhaust as the bus pulled away, with a stream of people running after, leaping for the door, hanging on for dear life or being pulled to safety from someone inside.

As we waited in big clouds of exhaust, instead of finding any humor in the situation, I was getting sour on this whole escapade, on Delhi, already sour on India. How hard could it be just to find and get on the #505 bus.

An Indian woman standing beside me smiled and asked where I was going. "Qutab Minar." I had to repeat it a few times before she understood me.

She asked if I was Christian (yes), and would I celebrate Christmas in India? I didn't know about that, where I'd be or if I'd celebrate it. My plans hadn't made it that far into the calendar yet.

As we waited, a bus pulled up and stopped, still half in the street, and the woman said, "This bus goes to Qutab Minar! Come!" So we ran, with a dozen other people, and tried to crowd in the doorway of an already full bus. People were pulling me in, and pushing me from behind, when the woman, who had squeezed on ahead of me, said, "No Qutab Minar! Not this one!"

So I bulled my way backwards and off, even as the bus started to roll on, and said, "Thank you!" to the woman, though I don't know if she could hear me in the crush.

As we kept waiting, I let Anneli do all the asking, because by now I was tired of all this business just trying to find a ride to Qutab Minar, and I didn't care if I ever got to see the damn thing anyway.

When we were just on the verge of giving it all up for a relaxing pot of coffee in a café somewhere, which sounded a whole lot better than what we were doing, an honest to goodness 505 bus pulled up! A crowd of people sprinted for the bus, Anneli was trying to confirm with the driver, and I saw what looked like the bus lieutenant leaning out a window. Most buses in Nepal and India had a driver and what I called a lieutenant, who usually rode the bus near the back door, and who could communicate to the driver, "All clear, go!" by banging on the side of the bus. "You go to Qutab Minar?" I hollered to him above the gunning engine.

"Yes, Yes! Get on!" We shoved our way onto the totally packed bus and were sucked further into the crowded innards by helping hands. Where there was absolutely no more room, two more Indian women squeezed in beside me and we all smiled in our discomfort.

Anneli and I were both standing, smashed against and between seats, facing out with our backs to the aisles, which were stuffed with about three to four people for each row, in addition to the lines of four seats stuffed with eight people. Incredibly, at each subsequent stop, we kept picking up more people – and *more* people - until there were five or six in each pair of seats. I thought a Nepali bus ride was something to write home about, but no, a local Nepali bus ride was like riding Super Executive First Class compared to this bus ride in Hell!

I was squished so hard from behind (I wore my day backpack) that I had to shove back, bracing against the windows, to keep from getting crushed against the windows.

But that wasn't the climax of the bus ride. *That* was when some asshole laid his hand on my butt, and started to slide it into the crack of my ass! I didn't even think, I whipped my head around – as I couldn't move one inch to get away from him - and snarled, "KNOCK IT OFF!"

He didn't blink in recognition, pretending he had nothing to do with it, but his hand disappeared in an instant. My first instinct was to throw an elbow in his face, but I could not raise my elbows anyway. I was so angry and shocked and flabbergasted. What luck!

The bus lieutenant hollered over the ocean of heads to us that Qutab Minar was next, and as I had just gotten a seat next to Anneli I was rather reluctant to leave it. I had to laugh – a billion people were riding this bus, fighting for a handhold or foothold, I was even squooshed in my aisle seat, and Anneli sat next to me, squeezed in a vise grip, hunched over and daintily eating two of her leftover desserts from a dented box.

We shoved our way up the aisle toward the bus door, and the bus hawked and spat us out onto the pavement like everyone else, although at least the driver actually stopped. Good riddance to bus 505!

We walked into the Qutab Minar (it was free), and well, I had to admit, it was worth the hassle getting there.

The Qutab Minar is a 240-foot high red sandstone and white marble tower first begun in 1193 AD. At the foot of this tower is the Quwwat-ul-Islam Mosque, the "Might of Islam," the first mosque to be built in India. Also begun in 1193, it was built on the foundations of a Hindu temple, and it was built with pillars and other things obtained from demolishing "27 idolatrous temples."

The many pillars in the court are varied in style and in no particular rhyme or reason. The 23-foot high iron pillar in the courtyard was erected in the fifth century, and scientists still can't figure out how iron of such purity hasn't rusted for over 2000 years, and how they cast such good quality back then.

It's said that if you can encircle the pillar with your hands with your back to the pillar, your wish will be fulfilled. Anneli did it with me forcing her hands together, and there were too many other people crowded around for me to take my turn.

There are two tombs on the site, and this Ala-ud-din, who made additions to the court and the Alai Darwaza gateway, got this brilliant idea to build a second identical Qutab Minar, only twice as high! The tower was only up to 88 feet high when he died, and nobody wanted to continue it.

A few foreigners and some Indians wanted to take our pictures, Anneli especially, I guess as souvenirs. One Indian snuck up and stood beside Anneli as she was waiting for his friend to snap their picture (the sneaky photo bomb before anybody had coined that phrase). I've heard the Indians just like to have their pictures taken with foreigners (us), although God knows what they tell their buddies back home at the pub. One white woman stood with two happy Indian kids for a picture taken by the happy parents.

When we left, the sun was dropping close to the horizon, and a rickshaw man kindly pointed us to where the bus would stop. We waited only 10 minutes until a 505 bus pulled up, and like a bunch of pros, we sprinted for the bus and jumped on and shoved inwards with the rest of the Indian passengers.

The fare was one rupee, and these public bus rides are indeed worth one rupee! If the ride to Qutab Minar was a bus ride in Hell, this return was Beyond Hell.

It started out not too bad, and a seat even opened up and some kind men made sure that I got a seat, although I was pretty squashed even sitting down. But I wasn't complaining because there were now suddenly a thousand people on the bus.

Anneli asked me on the way to Qutab Minar, "How many people do you think are on this bus, 80?" A good possibility. Now there had to have been 100 or more, though surely it was a thousand. The lieutenant bus man tapped me on the shoulder. "Connaught Place?"

I said "Yes," and he pointed, indicating the stop was coming up, and I had to exit forward - no way! Impossible!

I told Anneli to start pushing forward, and she couldn't move either, but we both started shoving ahead, just like the natives do, bending people over seats, sticking our armpits in faces, and stepping on feet because there was absolutely no vacant floor space.

The bus stopped when I hadn't shoved but two seat rows forward, then it moved on. I couldn't see a thing, with layers of people on both sides of me, and arms up in the air holding onto straps, and I thought, oh hell, we missed the stop.

Anneli was somehow well ahead of me, and I pushed and elbowed and shoved, and suddenly I had wedged myself so tight, so very tightly among people that I couldn't *move*. Not forward, not back, I couldn't see a thing, could barely glimpse Anneli close to the door, I was being squashed, I suddenly saw images in my head of people being crushed to death and trampled, and panic

33

washed over me in a wave.

I was racked with two spasms where I tried to throw myself loose, tried to get out – Oh God let me out – I clamped my mouth shut so I wouldn't scream. I remember now the same kind of rising panic when I almost drowned once. What saved me was the fresh air (if you can call any of this exhaust shit fresh) coming in the windows.

The only thing I could move was my head and I jerked it through the web of arms toward the windows, and sucked in long deep gulps and held them in, then breathed out slowly. The bus slowed for another stop coming up, and somehow with superhuman strength I shoved forward again, following the guy in front of me trying to do the same.

And then, thank you Lord, I was belched out of the bus onto the pavement, out of Beyond Hell back into Delhi, just thankful to be alive. I almost kissed the filthy cement! What a day! What a trip! Public buses in Delhi – NEVER AGAIN! I don't care if heaven is at the other end. No reward is worth that.

We had to wade back to and through the Main Bazaar, i.e. the zoo, with the same money changers, the same beggars, the same man pushing the same leg-less man in the cart, both of them moaning in raspy, anguished voices, "Hello! Memsahib! Memsahib!" and holding out their hands and reaching out to touch us. If their hands didn't touch me the ragged voices did. The same fruit vendors shoved apples in our faces; the same kids grabbed at us; the same men always dug in their crotches rearranging their furniture with one hand as casually as they smoked their cigarettes in the other hand and stared at us.

At the hotel, Anneli changed to her Indian dress – she enjoys this as much as I enjoy the eating – and we bravely plunged back outside to go eat in the crowded Leema Café, crowded mostly with Israelis. As soon as we were finished, the waiter wanted to run us off since plenty of people were lined up inside waiting to sit at tables.

But by golly, we'd had a rough day, and neither of us was ready to be rushed out the door yet. I ordered a milk coffee, which the waiter wasn't happy about, and when he brought my coffee, then Anneli ordered a coffee, and he said "Sorry, not possible." Anneli scolded him, and he got so mad he yelled for a coffee for her.

I couldn't drink my coffee any faster than I was sipping it – had to be savored you know. Anneli took her time also, and meanwhile we were joined at our table - unasked, the waiter had just pointed to an empty seat at our table - by a guy who gave off rather bizarre wavelengths. I couldn't pinpoint it, but he reminded me of the entire punk band Devo. And he preferred to sit with his walkman earphones on instead of speaking to us, and he got his food thrown at him – I guess the waiter was so mad at us that he was mad at this guy too for just sitting with us.

When we finished our drinks and finally decided to get up and leave, I told one gal in the waiting line, "Sorry we took so long."

She said "Oh, no problem, I saw how he was harassing you two."

I said "Yea, I was going to order another coffee."

She laughed "You should have!"

As it was, he didn't charge us for a tea, and we felt no compulsion to remind him.

It was just one of those Delhi Days.

AGRA

December 6

We opted for an 11:00 AM train to Agra so we wouldn't have to get up early. Good thing, since disco music blared from one radio and screeching Indian music from another until 2:30 AM, then it started up again at around 5 AM. When people in the hotel started hollering at 7:30 AM that was the sign it was time to get up.

After another good breakfast of things I did not order, we finished our packing at the hotel. Anneli's pack is half the size of mine, and mine is stuffed to the brim. It's heavy too, and doesn't fit around my hips right, so my back and shoulders have to carry all the weight. I'm not sure what all I have in my pack and why I thought I had to bring it all!

When we left the hotel, the desk guy told me, "Bye Noni." He calls me Noni, because I look like a Noni from San Francisco.

The train station was crowded, and confusing, although there were some things written in English. We opted for the second class booking, non-reserved ride to Agra, but a tout intercepted us and sent us to a different counter. I preferred to ignore these people, expecting erroneous information or them asking for money, but he didn't ask for anything as he sent us to the second class reservations counter.

I told the lady we wanted to go on the Jelum Express at 10:50 to Agra. She nodded and said 39 rupees when I asked how much. We got our tickets, easy enough, and as we stood around wondering where to find our platform, a man stopped and asked us which train we wanted. "Jelum Express."

"Platform four, it leaves at 10:50," he answered and walked on.

First we looked for a bathroom, which, of course, was nowhere to be seen anywhere. We found a refreshment room upstairs, where Anneli asked for a bathroom, and the man pointed down the hall. We found them, two stalls, one locked, and the other one had a urinal in the front part and the toilet another door beyond that. But it was clean enough and it was a toilet! While we took turns, two big senior cops with bamboo sticks (no guns) came and chased out three people, hitting one with his stick.

At the platform we waited with a crowd of people, and the train pulled in at 10:35. The only cars we saw said Two Tier Sleeper, so we worked our way towards the train end, where it said the same thing. Another man asked us, "Where are you going?"

We said "Agra."

He pointed forward and said some numbers, so we swam back forward through waves of people. We found a man writing numbers on car placards, and Anneli asked him. He looked at a chart, "5-2 and 5-3, cars #11679."

Whatever exactly that meant, we did finally find the car, and climbing aboard, we took the first open two spaces we found. The padded (but not at all soft) two benches seated four each, with two more seats across the aisle. I sat by the window.

People passed by on the platform outside the train selling all manner of things - baskets, chains, food. Kids ran up to the windows begging. Inside the train car, up and down the aisle a one-armed beggar begged. A train attendant served food and instant coffee from a cart.

We shared our cubby with six Indians, one of them a woman. As we pulled out at 11:15, only 25 minutes late, I remembered all the headlines I'd seen of Indian train wrecks, killing dozens of people.

Inshallah, as the Arabic saying goes, If God wills it. You don't think about that anyway, once the train begins rolling, and you're on the train anyway, so no point in worrying about it. Outside it looked hot and dry, although it was green where crops were growing, and the air blowing in my half-open window was semi-cool.

The train rolled past shantytowns and tent and mud-dwelling villages, and the stench of sewage seeped into the train and settled around us.

After a while the men next to Anneli started a conversation with her, and all were eager to point out places in the *Lonely Planet* book for us to go all over India.

After two hours, the older couple sitting across from us pulled out a home-boxed lunch, and shared it with us, insisting we eat. They gave us each two chapatis, and a whole lid full of heavenly spiced veggies – peas, cauliflower, and a really spicy mango chutney made with hot chili and curry.

Then they shared their dessert, a sticky sweet soft donut that melted in my mouth. The man made us each eat two. I felt bad we were taking their food, but they insisted, and they enjoyed our pleasure.

The man even gave a begging boy wandering the aisles a chapati and veggies they had left over. Then they gave us each a banana. I wished we had something for them!

The man then joined in the conversation and offered advice, but I had a very hard time understanding his English accent, although Anneli had an easier time of it.

I wrote five postcards and looked at my India book a bit, but otherwise just relaxed, enjoying the peaceful train travel with a quiet, pleasant group.

We pulled into the first Agra station at 2:30, but I knew from my book that we wanted the second stop. There signs said "Agra cantonment," and the people pointed it out to us.

We said bye and thanked the couple again for lunch, and strapped on our packs, but we were slow, and didn't make it off the train before the new people started pushing in. So, we just plowed and elbowed our way out, dodging the elbows and knees from the incoming passengers.

Immediately upon stepping onto the platform a tout assailed us. I said no thanks and marched onward. He followed us all the way outside, and down the street a good five minutes.

The moment we stepped out of the front of the train station, we were *swarmed* with a cloud of cycle rickshaws and putt putt drivers. It was like being attacked by bees!

"Where you going! Get in! Tourist Rest House? Taj Mahal? Five rupees! Four rupees! Hello! Hello!" At least 20 people either pushing or driving their vehicles, tagged alongside, behind, or in front of us. I had to walk around several because they would stop and cut me off.

The first tout from the train station was still hounding Anneli and she was getting mad. We kept walking down the road, still followed by at least seven humans or vehicles, one guy saying, "Two rupees."

I finally said to Anneli, "You want to take this one for two rupees so they leave us alone?"

She agreed, so we climbed in, pissing off the other drivers. For two rupees he took us to the Tourist Rest House we asked for, and chatted with us along the way. "Where are you from? What do you do? How long you in India?"

A double room here with bath cost us 185 rupees (about $7). Anneli didn't like the room but it looked fine to me, after some of the places I'd stayed in, and they had a communal hot shower!

As Anneli signed us in – I stayed in the room – one guy hassled her about a tour and got her steamed because she said no several times and he wouldn't shut up.

I did have to go back and sign my name too, and two people hassled me, but I shortly said no thank you, and they quit.

I ran to the shower first, and had a wonderful quick hot hair wash. By the time Anneli took one, there was little hot water left.

Coffee was the next important order of business, so we ordered hot pots of tea and coffee in the nice little courtyard with a few people and hundreds of flies.

I spoke to a girl at the next table, LeeAnn, who was traveling India alone, and I asked her when the Taj Mahal closed.

"Dusk?" she shrugged. She pulled up a chair and joined us.

"It's now closed," said the waiter. "5:00 closes." We decided to go anyway after we finished our drinks.

We decided we'd pay only three rupees for a ride to the Taj. Five people swarmed us the minute we stepped out of the hotel. "15 rupees," said one.

"Three rupees," we said and walked on. Some kept following us, and some went down to five rupees.

One man in a putt putt said, "OK three rupees," but when we got in and sat down he said, "Five rupees."

We said, "No, three rupees!"

"OK three rupees we stop at such and such."

LeeAnn ordered, "NO! STRAIGHT to the Taj." LeeAnn was familiar with the routine and knew how to handle it.

He said, "One stop..." so we climbed right back out and started walking. It was the principle of the thing, you know.

We walked down to The Mall street, and turned left, a few more putt putts following, a man yelling "10 rupees!"

We said, "Two rupees," and he said we couldn't possibly walk that far, two rupees, what, we were nuts. More people tried us, and a cycle tried us.

"Two rupees," we said. We did just wish they'd leave us alone, but ignoring them did nothing to stop the offers. "Two rupees each," he said. Nope, we kept walking.

It was darkening now, but not a lot of road traffic or foot traffic. Finally the cycle guy, still following us, said, "OK two rupees," and the three of us piled on, with me sitting on LeeAnn's knee.

I felt bad at times, watching these guys pedal their butts off for eight cents, but they could always go on to the next customer, (and they did), and we still paid more than the native Indians.

He dropped us off near the entrance to the Taj, and didn't dispute the two rupees I handed him. By now it was totally dark, but we thought we'd at least get a glimpse of it lit up through some gates.

But the Taj Mahal was still open! It was 6:15, and it closed in 45 minutes, and it was Friday, so it was free. And there were very few people so it was quiet! The monument wasn't lit up at all – the only light was reflected from the city lights on the haze, which the marble white absorbed - but it was still incredible. We walked in near solitude up to it, and it grew bigger and more magnificent the closer we got.

The Mughal emperor Shah Jahan commissioned the Taj Mahal as a tomb for his favorite wife, Mumtaz Mahal. It was built between 1631-1643 AD by 20,000 workers, though extra work continued another 10 years.

We walked up the steps and had to leave our shoes at the entrance, and as we walked up onto the main level, a man with a flashlight pulled us inside. "I'm not guide, I'm watchman!"

He took pride in his job, and showed us some incredible inlaid detail work of tiny pieces of garnet and jade forming flowers in the marble. The symmetry of the building was exquisite, and the fine echoes in the chamber saintly.

Then a "priest" standing by two tombs with a candle and flowers and big bright 100-rupee and 50-rupee notes laying on the altar beside him asked for money for the poor. Would it really go to the poor? But I put down a two rupee note, because how could you not in this magical place?

As we walked out of the chamber, the watchman told us the Taj Mahal opened at 6 AM tomorrow. We walked unspeaking in the dark, in socks on white marble, around this huge silent white memorial with its four 130-foot high minarets staring down at us in peaceful silence. It wasn't ghostly or eerie; it was tranquil and majestic!

On either side of the Taj Mahal are twin red sandstone mosques. I remembered my handy flashlight in my pack, and we walked inside the western mosque, also silent, and empty, and also peaceful and splendid in the dark, with only the strong beam of my little flashlight disturbing anything.

And what's most amazing is there could have been another Taj Mahal, a tomb for Shah Jahan himself, a negative image of the Taj in black marble. But his son Aurangzeb put a stop to that by imprisoning him in the Red Fort. Shah Jahan was eventually entombed in the Taj Mahal, laying forever at rest in the afterlife with his adored wife.

We left the peaceful Taj Mahal for the final time, back into the maelstrom of Agra, besieged by rickshaw and putt putt drivers as we walked out the main entrance, but we managed to ignore them.

A man standing in the doorway of the Nice Point Restaurant beckoned to us. It had a Lonely Planet circle painted on it, and indeed it was recommended in the book.

"Good food!" the man said. "If you don't like, you don't pay!" Well, my potato cheese curry was pretty bad, not one atom of curry in it, but the paratha was OK and dessert was interesting. The banana lassi was refreshing, and the cold pepsi was delightful, all for 27 rupees. So it was acceptable, and breakfast there looked promising.

Back at the hotel, I had the not-so-fun chore of studying the *Lonely Planet* to see how to get to Bharatpur, the bird sanctuary, tomorrow. Then I spent an hour writing in my journal, while I listened to rats under our floor – I was sure there were rats in our room!

< > < > < > < > < >

December 7

I should've known when I got up to pee at 3:30 AM, then heard the rats scurrying about our room ever afterward, keeping me awake until my alarm went off at 5 AM, that it wasn't going to be a good day. If the rats didn't keep me awake, the mosquitoes did, buzzing in my ears. I heard a horse wearing jingle bells go by three times in the night.

We finally got up at at 6:15 AM, and we started out toward

the Taj Mahal from the guest house at the same time LeeAnn and her friends did, swarmed, of course, by bikes and putt putts. After the usual arguing over prices, walking on, and more non-stop bargaining, after two blocks we climbed into a putt putt for two rupees.

Entrance today into the Taj Mahal was two rupees, and we walked in while the place was still bathed in a pre-dawn mist.

What an incredible monument. Simply magnificent. Every time I walked away from it and turned to look back on it, it was just as breathtaking as the first time I saw it. How was such an incredible work of art built 400 years ago?

The Taj Mahal is deservedly a UNESCO World Heritage Site, named as such in 1982.

I wandered around and took a whole roll of pictures (a film camera in those days), with no guides or shoe people to hassle me. It was one of the most peaceful 90 minutes I'd spent in India so far, and that included sleeping.

Afterwards, at the Nice Point restaurant we ate breakfast. I ordered toast and jam, muesli, and coffee, and while it took a long time to get my fruit curd muesli (with cornflakes) I got everything I ordered.

From then on, the day sucked hind tit. We had to rush back to our hotel to get packed and checked out by 10 AM, and we finished right on the button.

Our train to Bharatpur was not until evening, so we left our big packs in the train storage room and walked to the Agra Fort. We missed a turn, so we ended up walking down a busy road where apparently not many tourists walk.

"Hello! Hello! Sssst. Hey Baby." It had a bad vibe to it and it didn't feel pleasant. This was more harassment than hassle, and I was tiring of it.

As we arrived at the Red Fort, were approached by a cycle rickshaw. It wasn't 20 steps to the entrance to the fort. "Hello Red Fort? One rupee!" Was he serious? He was, but we all three laughed. We almost climbed in his rickshaw just to do it.

It cost two rupees to enter this UNESCO World Heritage

Site.

The Red Fort was a big interesting place where we walked around in peace, although it was so hazy we could barely make out the Taj Mahal just across the river. (The color of the Taj is fading due to acid rain from the terrible pollution in Agra and Delhi.)

As we walked out of the Fort, we were, as usual, swarmed again by offers of transport; we wanted to go to the Quality Restaurant for two rupees, but for two rupees they all wanted to take us to a different restaurant, or stop on the way at some shop where we would be unable to resist the terrific best prices.

The Quality Restaurant, recommended in the *Lonely Planet,* was totally *not* quality. It looked like a posh place, and the menu prices were high by any Indian standard. I ordered a veggie kofta, but did not want the boiled rice at the outrageous additional price of 18 rupees.

The waiter told me I needed to order rice. "No thanks," I said, "just the kofta."

He said "Sorry, not possible." What, not possible to serve without rice? Not possible to eat it without rice?

"Just the kofta," I insisted.

Then I got up to go to the toilet, where, wouldn't you know, an attendant was standing. He was holding five rupees, and tried to hand me a towel.

I said "No, no."

He said "No, it's alright," and said something about give if you like. Well I was crabby already today, and I didn't like, and I peed and washed my hands and face and even wiped my nose on the towel, walked out, and plopped the rag on the counter and walked back to my table. That was rude of me and it wasn't his fault, but I couldn't help myself. High food prices and a pay toilet in the restaurant!

The food came while Anneli was in the bathroom, (where she didn't pay either), and it was the smallest portion I'd ever been served anywhere. Maybe I should have gotten the mandatory rice.

We stalked out of there and walked across the street to look for a pastry shop recommend in *Lonely Planet*, having to step around and weave through the swarming bike rickshaws.

Instead of finding the pastry shop we found a persistent girl begging, and an even more persistent woman begging, exposing her baby's burned butt. "Madam money! Madam baksheesh! *Madam!*"

We retrieved our packs from the hotel, and headed for the Idgah train station indicated on our map in the *Lonely Planet*. We'd written this station and the 5 PM departure time down from somewhere.

When we were swarmed by putt putts, "15 rupees for Idgah," we laughed and walked on with our packs to the Idgah train station. Only the laugh was on us because we started out the wrong direction.

The day got worse. We did not make good decisions. Following our map, we cut over on a road to the left, which was covered in slimy black oozy mud, until we came to a dead end, and had to walk all the way back out, and back past our guest house. Back to where we started from.

It was five minutes until 5:00 now, and *then,* of course, no cycle rickshaws or putt putts even stopped for us. We kept bullheadedly heading for this Idgah train station as indicated on my map, although I said we'd never make a 5 PM train.

Anneli said, "Oh I'm sure we will. The last train left 20 minutes late."

Well I was getting quite cranky now, as the further we walked, the heavier my pack got, and the more hassles we got: "Hello! Sssssst! Hey baby! Pssshhh! Hello!" And it was not a friendly hello from the men. It was a harassing, slightly threatening hello.

We walk on, and on; it was getting dark; we should have been there by now; it was now 5:30 PM. We asked a traffic cop, and he didn't know, then yes, he did know, and bobbing his head in the Indian way that means inexplicably either yes or no, he indicated down this road; we kept walking, many more hassles,

I hate traveling, I said to myself, I hate India, I hate Agra most of all.

We took another road, which turned out to be a dead end, and a man directed us back; we backtracked, I was sweating, there was no sign of a damn train station or even a train track anywhere; we came to another fork in the road, totally helpless. No rickshaws even approached us in this sketchy neighborhood.

A group of boys started gathering around us, they wouldn't answer our "Idgah?" questions, or they pretended not to understand. They started moving in closer, and finally one boy pointed up a fork of the road.

Anneli started that way. I said "No, we're going to the Main station, we're lost, have no map, we don't even know if the train leaves from Idgah, we don't even know if there is a station, it's way past time, and it's getting dark, and I'm tired of these stares and catcalls." Not to mention I was getting scared with the bad vibes and all the men and boys surrounding us in the dark night.

They left us alone and stayed behind as we turned and walked back a very long way. One man walking on the street asked us where we were going, and he called a cycle over to take us back to the Main Station for five rupees. He knew this was a neighborhood we did not belong in. Thank you, mister Guardian Angel. Thank you God.

But the night wasn't over yet, and neither were the trials.

We got to the Main Station at 6 PM, where the friendly man at tourist information scolded us and said there is no Idgah train station, but there was a morning and evening train, leaving for Jaipur at 8:20 PM from the Agra Fort station, and it stopped in Bharatpur on the way.

So we walked back out of the station, now of course swarmed by rickshaws offering to take us to the Agra Fort train station for 20 rupees! One offered eight rupees, so 30 minutes of pedaling got us to the grubby Agra Fort station where we bought second class unreserved (another big mistake) "seats" for 13 rupees each.

The train was already waiting. We had no idea which cars were second class unreserved, and we walked up and down the train several times. I found and asked a stationmaster in his office if this was the train to Jaipur that stopped at Bharatpur, and he said yes.

Which car do we get on? He pointed to one. We tried it but another train man on board said wrong car. I said "But which one?"

He jumped off and said, "Come!" We chased after him to a couple of *packed* cars – six people to the benches made for four, no room for luggage, five men sitting on the floor in front of the toilet – which made all my urge to pee go away, and men sitting in the aisles.

There was absolutely no other place to go, so I plopped my bag right in the aisle and sat on the floor by a sadhu. Anneli plopped her bag next to mine in the aisle and sat on the other side of it. We were lucky to get these ticketed "seats" on the floor.

I sat there stonily, amidst hassling stares, wondering, why, oh why, did I have to travel through India. I hate this place.

The actual train ride wasn't so bad, and the sadhu even shared his burlap sack with me so I wouldn't have to sit right on the dirty floor. I wasn't terribly uncomfortable, and lots of people either had to stand or sit with half a butt cheek on a corner of the benches.

We thought it would take an hour, but after an hour passed, there was no sign of Bharatpur. The train had stopped a couple of times - maybe we had missed the stop. But no big deal - if worse came to worst, we could just get off at Jaipur after sitting and suffering six more hours, since Jaipur was our eventual major destination.

I asked in general if anyone knew which stop was Bharatpur. I was answered with another 10 minutes of silent staring and a few Hindi words which I didn't understand. Anneli tried asking, and finally, one man said, "In two stops," but you never know if they know what they're talking about, or if they know what we're talking about, or if they just want to be helpful.

47

After another long stop at an indecipherable station (words written in Hindi), it was 9:40 PM, and the man said, "Next stop, you'll be there at 10 PM."

Thank the lord, I thought, but Anneli sassed him, "No that's not possible. I'm sorry, it's not possible." She had had it up to her eyeballs, today, too. I had plenty of time sitting there on the dirty train floor among a crowd of legs and bare feet to think of how much I was currently fed up to my own eyeballs.

Next time the train slowed down I saw people reaching for things, and the sadhu stood up and mumbled Bharatpur.

I did see a "Bharatpur" sign in English out a window, so I told Anneli to be ready to shove out, because people were lined up outside waiting to shove in when the train rolled to a stop.

The door opened and instantly people erupted into the train door, Anneli couldn't go anywhere, I couldn't move, people were pushing and shoving and next thing I see right ahead of me is Anneli struggling madly, then slapping a man hard in the face!

Everyone saw it, everyone was shocked, but nothing like this man was! A guy behind us passed us and shoved his way out, and held a little path for us, like parting the Red Sea, but this lasted only two seconds.

But Anneli pushed forward and I shoved her from behind, and the sadhu pushed me, and we all spilled out and crashed onto the platform.

"What happened!?" I asked.

Well, the guy sitting half off the bench had been purposely brushing her or touching her since it was so crowded, and when she couldn't move while trying to get out, he grabbed her butt! And she automatically slapped him.

But our trials still weren't quite over.

We looked in the *Lonely Planet*, and we picked the Kuhmer Gate area, where four hotels were listed. The first rickshaw told us 20 rupees.

I said no and walked on, and he said OK, 10 rupees, and I didn't argue.

Anneli said, "I think five rupees each is too much." I was

on the verge of cracking up mentally. What did she want, to walk? It was late, neither of us had a hotel on our crude maps, so we really had no idea how to get to Kuhmer Gate. "I'll pay it!" I said.

So we got cycled in the dark, and arrived at this dumpy Kuhmer Gate area. The first hotel just looked too expensive for the likes of us. The next hotel was mentioned in the book, and the unfriendly man showed us a 150-rupee double room. Way too expensive but I said OK with me.

Anneli didn't like it. I bit my tongue and we left that hotel and walked on down the road. I spotted another one mentioned in the book, the Hotel Avadh. This smooth-talking guy I took an instant dislike to showed us a dirty double room with common bath for 90 rupees, "but I think this is not good enough for you. I think you want double deluxe." That was with a bath, for 140 rupees.

I didn't like the hotel, period, but it was 10:30 PM and I had reached my limit of sanity and tolerance. I said OK, and Anneli, equally fed up with this day and this time and place, said "Yea! Fine!" and we took the deluxe.

But, this bad day was *still* not over. No rats in our room, but we noticed some loud, obnoxious, screeching, monotonous Hindi music out the window, a window that would not completely close. That wasn't unusual in itself, but as we sat dog-tired and finally unwinding, we realized this was an outdoor concert – or was it? We had seen strange bright lights from the rickshaw which only dawned on me then they could've been concert lighting in a stadium. But here in Bharatpur?

I was exhausted, but I had to try a shower. I had turned on the switch earlier but the water heater light still wasn't on; then I saw the plug. Well of course it won't heat up if it's not plugged in, how silly. I plugged this big ancient three-pin plug into the socket and turned the switch on, and a red light grinned at me. Ahh, I thought, at least I'll feel a little better with a hot shower.

After this bad day my head was massively clogged again, I had a raw throat, and my neck glands on both sides were swollen and sore. Will this cold never end?

I tried the shower again, and you guessed it, cold water – that figures. I had another cold splash-off bath, and they aren't refreshing.

It took me 15 minutes just to jot notes in my journal from this abominable day. I crawled in bed at 11:30 PM after setting the alarm for 6 AM, with the music still blaring away. People living any closer must have been deaf. The music was monotonous and seemed to be repeating itself in a very short loop. The same notes, over and over and over and loud. Lucky Anneli had earplugs.

Suddenly at 12:30 AM – the music stopped! The silence was stunning. Still I couldn't sleep, too many things today, too much hassle, everything kept rushing at me. I hate India, this totally sucks, I hate it all. I'm not ready to leave for Thailand yet; I'm waiting until I find out if I can visit my friends in Madras, but Thailand is a definite open option, one that will be so much easier than India.

Just as I dozed off, you guessed it, the music began blaring again. Same screeching, same repetitive chords, same volume. I had no humor left in me and I lay there, just *done.*

BHARATPUR

December 8

Somehow I slept. I know the music continued all night because I heard snatches of it throughout the night, as if glancing at something that was always there.

The alarm went off at 6 AM, and though I felt my usual morning death-warmed-over self, I popped right up, used the toilet, dressed and packed before Anneli got up. I wanted to leave this stupid place behind.

Last night I had tried to unplug the three-pin plug of the water heater. I didn't get it unplugged, but I did rip the whole panel out of the wall. Shit! I tried to fix it this morning, but it popped right back out, so I said the hell with it and hoped they wouldn't notice.

Then I accidentally knocked an empty soda bottle on the floor and shattered that; I threw away the big pieces and kicked the shards under the bed, because I was sure we'd get charged for that.

Anneli finally got up, and we walked out at 6:30 AM and dropped the key at the desk. The man had Anneli sign again, and sent his assistant up for a "room check." As if we were going to steal something! I think I preferred the hotel with rats in my room.

Our goal today was the Bharatpur bird sanctuary, but my heart just about was not in this anymore. I couldn't imagine how looking for a few birds was going to be worth all this cumulative hassle. But I certainly was not going to stay in Bharatpur again, nor travel back to Agra, not for any reason. Bharatpur bird sanctuary could not possibly be as awful.

Outside we were soon approached by a cycle. For four rupees, this completely non-English-speaking man (we had held fingers up to indicate rupees) cycled us to the main gate of the bird sanctuary (stopping to ask another cycler where we were going), smiled and nodded when we handed him four rupees, and then we walked to the Saras Hotel for breakfast. We also signed there for 20-rupee dorm beds, dropped our packs off, then ambitiously rented bikes for 20 rupees for a half day.

Also a UNESCO World Heritage Site, the Bharatpur Bird Sanctuary (nowadays known as Keoladeo National Park) was originally a royal hunting reserve in the mid-1800s for the Maharajahs and the British. The 11 square miles of a combination of wetlands, woodland swamps, woodlands, and dry grasslands is home to more than 360 bird species, and is one of the world's most important breeding and feeding grounds for birds. The rare Siberian Crane overwinters here.

For owl fans, the spotted owlet lives here. Not the same species as our endangered spotted owl in the U.S., this is a smaller owl that has more of a facial resemblance to a burrowing owl.

The bird sanctuary was declared protected in 1971, established as a national park in 1982, and designated a World Heritage Site in 1985. It's an artificial wetland in a natural depression, and its continued existence is always threatened by water being diverted for famers. This park turned out to be simply superb, in so many ways.

The 25-rupee entrance fee was for non-Indians. Once we pedaled in, and once we got to the swamps and starting seeing and hearing the billions of birds, I started to relax, thinking that traveling in India was starting to look up.

I'd never been much of a biker, but here everything was flat and wind-less, and I finally started enjoying the pretty quiet pedaling, stopping wherever we felt like it to sit and watch the plethora of birds – herons, cranes, storks, cormorants, sandpipers, ducks, kingfishers, parrots, eagles, bright blue birds, plus deer, monkeys, mongoose, civets, jackals, and so much more.

We pedaled to the west park boundary, where we saw some Indians harvesting grass in the park. The dozen women and kids all stopped their work and stared. The kids yelled, "Hello!" in a demanding way. We yelled back, "Hello!"

The bumpy ride along the dry desert scrub where we saw nothing but Brahma cattle was uninteresting (cattle grazing was banned in the park in 1982, which caused violent clashes between farmers and the government), but eventually we got back onto a trail through swamps, where we spied a spotted deer.

We ran into a friendly trio of Indians asking us if we saw deer, and which birds, so we were able to act as tour guides for them. Another friendly group took Anneli's picture. One group took a picture of me with a guy who put his arm around my shoulders, and I put his bright blue cap on and made them laugh.

We stopped at the canteen for a snack of milk biscuits and a good cup of tea. I was finally starting to de-stress, for the first time since I'd arrived in India. Here, there was no constant tension from every direction. The air was clean and clear, the only noise the soft voices of Mother Nature.

After pedaling some more miles on quiet roads along creeks and forest, we returned to the hotel and our dorm room, which looked amazingly clean, quiet, and spacious.

At the restaurant we ordered lunch, and a waiter we subsequently affectionately named Goofy was ready to clear our table, "finished?" before we ever got our rice or Anneli's main dish. He did everything with a theatrical flourish that made us all laugh.

Afterwards we sat outside on the little lawn, sipped more tea, and just chilled. There was nowhere we had to be, nothing we had to bargain for, no noise we had to steel ourselves against. It was beautiful here.

We sat outside until it got cooler and near dusk, then we went inside for more milk coffee. Goofy tried to rush us, but when he saw we were parked there for the evening, he gave up and left us alone.

An Aussie returned from a local bus trip to Deeg, and he sat down and joined us. I thought he spoke Aussie, but I knew I also heard a Scottish inflection, but he definitely didn't sound English, so I asked. He was from Scotland and had lived in Australia for several years. We sat and talked over dinner.

<> <> <> <> <>

December 9

I slept so well, and I felt so awful with my cold when I woke up, I seriously considered staying in bed until noon.

The alarm went off at 6:30 but Anneli ignored it, and Peter, who'd moved into our dorm room, also ignored it, so I dozed again until 7 AM, when I thought I'd better get us all up.

We left the room by 7:30, and walked in the cool crisp morning fog to the park entrance, down to where boats waited on the edge of the swamp.

The sun had risen, but it was only an orange fuzzy ball hanging in the haze. It cost the three of us only 50 rupees together for an hour, and our guide started poling us down a reedy canal.

Once we got into the swamps and into the birds, we were so far from the madding crowd of India that we'd entered another planet. Our guide was a bit hard to understand, but what I couldn't translate, Anneli could, and vice versa. He really knew his birds, and was good at spotting them and pointing them out to us.

The water was remarkably clear, and we saw the occasional frog on a lily pad, and fish ripples around our boat. Our guide would quietly pole as close as he could to the birds for pictures. He really enjoyed what he was doing, and he knew a lot about the breeding habits, which birds migrated and from where, and he pointed out other animals in the park. I thought he had the best job in the world.

We saw a few deer and antelope, and so many birds,

much more so than from the road: storks, cranes, sandpipers, kingfishers, ducks and more ducks, even an eagle.

Our guide kept us out over an hour. This was one of the best places I'd ever been, even worth the hassles and harassment it took to get here. It was so calm and peaceful and *quiet*. I wished I could spend the rest of my three weeks in India in this boat.

JAISALMER

"Best camel trek! Best quality!"

That's what they all say, so we took the easy option and signed up for a three-day-and-night camel trek in the desert outside of Jaisalmer with the Deepak Tourist Bungalow where we were staying.

Anneli, my German traveling partner for the last week, was rather crabby about it, saying she wanted to compare other trekking companies. "Go ahead," I said, "go visit some others and let me know what you find out."

But she went along with the rest of us, because we liked our bungalow, and it was just easier than shopping around, because nobody would proclaim, "We have the worst trek! Sign up with us!"

And, I mean, think about it. You stay at one hotel and you buy a camel trek offered by another hotel? That's just bad protocol, bad travel karma. India was already full of travel challenges. You didn't need just one more thing to come back and bite you in the ass.

I did think the price was a little steep at 700 rupees ($28 per day), but that was my budget backpacker mind talking!

Anneli and I had met up with Tom and Malcolm and James and Dave, riding the same train from Jodhpur to Jaisalmer in western India together, and we'd all headed to this same guest house.

India is much more fun (and tolerable) if you're traveling with a group of like-minded backpack travelers. The highs and lows and joys and disappointments can be shared and carried on other shoulders if it becomes too much for a single person to bear at some point. And in India, those "some points" came often. The three boys, and Anneli and I, often leaned on each other for different things throughout the week we spent together.

Camel trekking was one of the popular backpacker tourist activities in this western desert region of India. The Thar desert, or the Great Indian desert, stretched over 77,000 square miles in western India's state of Rajasthan, and spilled over the border of eastern Pakistan.

Camels would be our transport, and we'd get to visit a few small villages on the trek, and sleep out on sand dunes under the stars.

<> <> <> <> <>

Day 1

"We will leave at 10 AM" became 11, which became 12 noon, but after two weeks in India, by then we knew not to get too excited about time schedules. Most of the Indian trains miraculously ran more or less on time (I never figured that out - it was before the internet and online scheduling, and train ticket clerks still wrote things on pieces of paper), but everything else ran on "India time."

Eventually, eight of us - the four boys, Anneli and I, and two people we hadn't met yet, Michelle and her husband Dave (known as Husband Dave on the trek, since we already had a Dave), stuffed ourselves and our backpacks (and, in Tom's case, a cricket bat) in back of the guesthouse jeep and we headed westward, with our hotel owner and guide, Danesh, and a driver.

First stop was for tea at a little village and, as white-skinned people, we were all stared at, as we usually experienced all over India. In the next village where we stopped, I followed Tom and Dave on a mini-walk through this desert village. I was a major hit with my Canon film camera. The kids fought over looking through the viewfinder, and trying to take pictures. And they all wanted their pictures taken. All 15 boys lined up in a perfect line and posed stiffly for a shot.

The boys followed us around closely, always reaching out and requesting to look through my camera when I took a picture, to see what I was seeing through the viewfinder.

Very few women were out and about, unless they were carrying pots on their heads. All of them wore bright, colorful saris - such a stark contrast to the dull uniform tan landscape of sand and huts. They ignored us, going about their work with purpose.

Tom and Dave and I joined the others inside a villager's hut and drank tea, surrounded by three dozen Indians, mostly kids. Anneli and I seemed to be most fascinating in the village. We were mobbed by a tight group, both kids and adults. Anneli had dark hair and she was tall and striking. They all just stood and stared, and smiled, and stared, and pointed to Anneli's wristwatch.

I took many pictures (asking Danesh for permission), and not once did I hear, "Give me one pen!" or "Hello one rupee!" as I did all over Nepal and in Delhi. The Nepalese kids and Indian city kids knew tourists were vending machines for handing out pens and a rupee or two; these rural Indian children were not yet used to so many tourists who always had expendable goodies in their pockets.

Back on the road, we didn't seem to have time to stop for lunch, so Danesh supplied us with a few packs of cookies. I loved riding in the open jeep through the desert, sometimes on a bad rough road, bouncing us around in our seats, sometimes in the smooth sand. There is just something soothing about moving from somewhere to somewhere else, by vehicle, boat, or train, on land or water, and not being hassled.

The desert here was mostly flat sand with scrub brush. As most deserts go, it can be brutally hot in the summers here, but December was a pleasant (and bearable) time to visit western India.

After a few hours, we arrived at Danesh's place in the

SOMEWHERE ELSE

desert where we would start the camel trek the next morning.

One of the turbaned guides brought out a saddled camel. These one-humped dromedaries made up 94% of the world's camels. They are still used in Asia and Africa as work beasts, providing transport, and as livestock, providing textiles, milk, and meat. Camels can go up to 10 days without water in very hot conditions, and they can tolerate a wide range of body temperature. They can survive eating what amounts to thorns on bushes. Camels originated in America, and crossed into Asia over the Beringia land bridge during the ice ages, and while over time they disappeared in North America, they were eventually domesticated in Asia.

I'd ridden plenty of horses. Most of them, if handled respectfully, didn't mind being ridden and worked. They could be very affectionate and attuned to humans. I had no idea what camels were like.

Michelle tried out it out first, awkwardly climbing aboard the kneeling camel, and hanging on for dear life as it lurched to its feet, during which much giggling ensued, from all of us tourists and the guides. Then I took my turn climbing aboard and Anneli got on behind me. Our camel was crying or whining or howling, a strange unfamiliar animal call. I didn't know if that was normal or if he was protesting being experimented on as the guide led us around.

I loved it, it was like a horse, only much bigger and more vocal! They are such fascinating beasts. We scratched his head and neck after we dismounted – do camels like that or not? I couldn't tell. He blinked his big brown eyes with big lashes at us whether we scratched him or not. Camels have two sets of long, thick eyelashes which angle downward, to protect against sand and the bright desert light. They also have three sets of eyelids, additional protection against ever-present and often-blowing sand.

While Danesh and his camel guides started organizing the cooking for dinner, we tourists got a small cricket game going - or rather Tom, from Great Britain, got us all started

59

on a cricket game. He was completely obsessed with this silly game. He'd coerced several of us into playing in Jaisalmer where a number of Indians joined us. I'd seen the game on TV and understood it not a whit; playing it didn't help my understanding at all. I just stood where Tom said to stand, and did what he told me to do.

When I 'bowled' this time I hit the stump and struck the guy out, which, by Tom's reaction, was exactly what I was supposed to do. He was quite impressed, and said so several times. Two of the Indians were impressed and said something to me in Hindi. I accepted all the praise with graceful humility, as if it were my due, "Thank you, thank you!" as if I had planned all that, but of course the accuracy was completely accidental on my part! Normally I can't hit the side of a barn standing ten feet away.

When it was dinner time we Americans were rather relieved the game was over, giggling again about the incomprehensible point of the pastime, which prompted a glare from Tom. He said, "Despite your good playing, I detect a *decided* lack of enthusiasm for the game." I shrugged noncommittally.

We were all trying, for Tom's sake, as I really thought that spreading the joys of playing cricket around the world for him was likened unto spreading world peace. Amen. We were making his vacation. The Indians everywhere greatly enjoyed playing it with us. Music is the universal language among people around the world; apparently cricket is the sports equal.

We were joined by another tour group returning from their three-day camel trek, and they said it had been great, though the guys said two days on a camel was plenty enough for them, as they directed their gazes downward.

After a meal of spicy veggies, rice and chapattis, and awful hot sweet tea, we all walked in the moonlight to the dunes where we'd be sleeping under the stars, a ten-minute walk away. Anneli, Husband Dave, Michelle, and I were the last ones, and we weren't sure where we were going, though it was so light with the over-half moon shining on the sand, we could always see the dunes ahead of us.

Arriving at the dunes, we found the others, picked out our mattresses on the sand, and trickled toward the campfire circle where the camel men were building a bonfire. Musicians materialized out of the darkness, and we were joined by 20 local Indians who sat outside the light of the fire watching and listening silently, just their faces lit by the flames.

Two men played bagpipe-like flutes, and a kid played a pair of sticks and belted out songs at the top of his voice. Another boy sang solos. An old man played a Jew's harp or jaw harp, like nothing I'd ever seen or heard before. Held in his mouth, he plucked a tine and changed the shape of his mouth to change the tones. Several of the Indians danced by the fire.

The songs and dances must go back hundreds or thousands of years; this form of entertainment is the same now as it was then, around a same fire under the same moon. Music, the universal language, indeed.

I stayed up until I couldn't keep my eyes open anymore – we all had a nip or two of some potent local desert whiskey – then I crawled under my blanket on my mattress on the sand under the star-spangled sky of the Indian desert night. The last thing I remembered was the music of the old man's jaw harp lulling me to sleep.

<> <> <> <> <>

Day 2

What an incredible peaceful night, sleeping on the sand dunes under the stars in Rajasthan! The moon set after 2 AM, and I briefly opened one eye to look for shooting stars, but I couldn't stay awake.

I woke at 7 AM, facing a strip of glowing maroon sky on the eastern horizon. I sat up and listened to the silence, watching the sky shift to purple, to golden. It was cool, and absolutely still. Nothing else smells like the morning desert in India.

People slowly awoke, and Danesh arrived with a camel pulling a cart to carry the first group back for breakfast. Malcolm and I hopped in so we could eat earlier.

Breakfast was: sugar. Sugar with a little tea, sugar in the jam on toast, sugar on the porridge and milk. Plenty of sugar to start our morning camel trek right! The others arrived and I scarfed more toast with sugar.

We were ready to set off on our camel trek at 9:30. Our camel guides had the camels saddled and ready and the cart loaded. I chose to carry my small backpack containing my camera on the camel, hooked onto a ring. Danesh locked our big backpacks in a hut, known as the "schoolhouse," and most of the others left their cameras or water on the cart. I just hoped my pack didn't break from bouncing so much on the camel.

I got a young camel driver who hopped up behind me, kind of like a tandem sky-diver situation. Some of us might know how to ride horses, but we sure didn't know anything about steering or controlling these strange groaning beasts with reins attached to pegs in their noses.

Mounted high on our Ships of the Desert, we set off across the sand. Camels don't trot; they pace. It's a smooth, rocking gait, with their big padded feet gliding over the sand. When they're about to jog, the big head in front of your face starts a big rhythmic vertical bouncing, then the body follows. It made me giggle.

My kid tried to get me to put my feet in the stirrups, but I rode without, and after I said, "No" the second time, he didn't ask anymore.

After an hour of walking and jogging, seemingly from nowhere to nowhere, we arrived at a little lone hut and stopped and dismounted. Three young girls stared at us, while we stared at them. One was married, Danesh said, and she sure looked awfully young to be married. We asked Danesh if we could take their picture, and he said yes. We weren't the first tourists they'd seen, but we were something different from their daily grind of living life in a harsh desert. We wondered about their lives as they likely wondered about ours.

We learned how they dried wild grapefruit to get the seeds, which they can sell for medicinal value. It's also fed to cattle and goats and helps them produce buttermilk.

The next place we stopped was a Rajput caste so we had to get off our camels and approach on foot. This caste ("rajaputra" literally means "son of a king") denotes a higher social class in India. Since Danesh is Brahmin (of the highest Indian caste) he got permission for us all to come in.

We three girls removed our shoes and walked into the kitchen, and watched one woman make chapattis and one woman churn buttermilk. The men sat together in the main room and presumably had manly discussions.

They gave us a few chapattis to share, and also, as at the other hut, curd to try. I ate with just my clean right hand. (The left hand is considered unclean, the one you use for toilet activities.) Here we saw millet stacked to be shredded to obtain the seeds.

Most of us seemed to enjoy this interaction with the natives and they with us. And I loved riding these camels, as has been done for thousands of years.

Most of our camel drivers know in English only the words "camel," "good," and "very." "Camel good! Camel very good!" One by one they'd all break out into Hindi songs as we were riding across the desert.

We finally stopped for lunch at 1:30, meeting our camel cart and using one little spindly thorn tree for shade. It had to be 80 degrees now, with no breeze; I could only imagine this place in the summer. The flies were bad, and we sat and talked, waiting for hot chai and hot spicy food on a hot afternoon.

We ate the same spicy veggies and rice and rotis. Danesh told us, "In the desert we don't say chapatti. Here it is roti." But all of us ate decidedly less than the night before. James' stomach was still bad and he didn't eat, Michelle's was a bit iffy and she didn't eat, and my stomach was iffy so I ate little. Besides, it was hot, and hot spicy food on a hot day just isn't that appetizing.

Michelle made my day, nay, my whole trip, when she shared her stockpiled Nice cookies with us.

We mounted up again when a breeze popped up and it was markedly not so hot. We paced along, with my Kaloo ("camel") taking over the lead. We got to jogging so fast, as did Michelle and her driver behind us, we all laughed. Michelle got to bouncing so hard and so high she cracked her driver up, and between gasping laughs, she asked me how to hold herself down in the saddle. "Use your legs," I said, though I couldn't explain how.

My kid driver wouldn't let anybody pass us. Tom said, "I think your driver's trying to ride off into the sunset with you."

We all laughed, we tourists hollering, "Kaloo – good!" and our camel drivers yelling, "Camel – very good!"

Dave and I broke into songs, since the camel drivers were always singing; we belted out Jingle Bells and Country Roads Take Me Home and the Sound of Music and the Beatles, and they laughed at us.

Approaching evening we stopped at another hut, and poor Malcolm was so sore he refused to ride anymore and said he was going to walk the two miles we had left to get to our camping spot for the night.

Danesh got a bucket, Tom crawled down into the well and filled the bucket with fresh, cool water. Danesh poured it over Dave's head – it was refreshing after the heat and grit!

On behalf of Malcolm's agony, Danesh said we could sleep in the sand dunes up ahead instead of our spot two miles away, so we walked to the dunes, and our camel drivers led their camels away. It was a great pile of sand hills, with soft, cool sand, great to run and walk in, and a good 360-degree desert view.

We girls sat in the dunes under the half-moon light and watched the sun set as the boys played "kabaddi," a kind of tag/tackle team sport from ancient India that Danesh taught them.

Three Indian boys from nearby huts visited us, just squatting and watching. We must have been strange alien entertainment to their isolated lives.

Anneli broke open a good pack of cookies and gave the three boys one; they ate the cookies and then giggled and ran off.

Danesh came up to tell us dinner was ready at 7:30, although half of us were ready for bed. Malcolm and James stayed in their dune mattress beds, and the rest of us went down to the camel cart-cum-kitchen for a different dinner of rice and dal bhat with some type of tomatoes in it. It was, as usual, spicy, and filling like the veggies, but different.

We talked with Danesh about the cooperatives and the problems out here, and about the camel drivers, who all seemed to have great pride in their camels and in being guides. They joined us briefly, and showed Dave and Tom a type of wrestling, and then Tom and Dave demonstrated arm wrestling.

The head camel driver took on Dave, and while Dave grunted and struggled and sweated, the camel driver looked like he was relaxing with a beer in an easy chair. He was just toying with Dave, and when he was ready, he easily smacked Dave's arm down. Indians and American cheered alike, and Dave had the biggest smile of all of us.

The camel drivers then showed us some amazing feats of strength in acrobatics, then went back to their own campfire. We all walked back up to our dune beds at 8:30 and passed out under the stars.

<> <> <> <> <>

Day 3

I woke up once around 2 AM, after the moon had set, and I forced myself to stay awake and watch for shooting stars. After I counted two, I figured that was good enough and I fell back asleep.

I opened my eyes and lifted my head up at 7 AM to see the reddening line of sky creeping up the Rajasthan horizon, then crawled back under my blanket. It was cooler this morning but it felt great under the blanket. Sand gets in everything but it's not like ocean beach sand that sticks to you forever.

After another snooze, I sat up and again watched the sun rise in the silence, with the bleating of goats and cries of herders off in the distance. All across the sand around us were beetle tracks. Some even went underneath our mattresses, but nobody ever felt any beetles sharing their beds.

Danesh joined us on the dunes as everybody slowly crawled out from under their blankets, and our head camel driver brought us up a pot of tea to put on the small fire they built near us. Danesh had brought us a plate of toast and jam, of which I ate about half. It was easier to eat in the mornings when it was cooler.

Two F-16s buzzed over us to the east, and we saw them in the distance a few more times throughout the day, far ahead of their sound, and once very low to the ground on either side of us. It seemed so incongruous - modern high-tech war planes amid the slow, quiet, ancient ways of Indian herdsmen and huts. Pakistan, the border less than a hundred miles west, and India forever live on the edge of intolerance.

We mounted up and jogged along in the desert. Kaloo, carrying me and Barkat, my kid camel driver partner, took up the lead again. I think Kaloo likes his head scratched between his ears, because when we stopped I'd scratch him, and he didn't seem to mind. At least, he didn't toss me off or roll over on me or whack me with his long-necked head.

We stopped in a Muslim village; it was rich and strong, Danesh said. They owned sheep, camels, goats, and a few horses. Danesh translated to the men that I had racehorses. That wasn't quite true - I was just a groom on a racetrack - but the story sounded impressive to them so I let it ride. I was hoping to hop on one and ride, but I wasn't offered.

The horses were the Marwari breed, with the distinctive curled inward ears that touch on the tips. The breed originated in this desert of India around the twelfth century and excelled as a cavalry horse.

Danesh showed us around, then escorted us to the school

house, where we sat down on the floor with the kids just as if we were in class. The teacher taught us some Hindi writing. I learned to write my name, just like the kids learned to write. He 'taught' us the alphabet, which, aside from about six vowel sounds, there are 36 different consonant sounds. He says it's very easy, but I had my doubts. I scribbled my Hindi name all over my journal, just like kids were writing in their notebooks.

Then Danesh showed us the village store – very small but stocked with everything – food, clothing, soap, animal feed. He let us sample things. Then we were served curd to drink which was sour but refreshing, because it was cool and something other than warm water and the always-hot tea. Danesh also passed out rotis, and, of course, hot chai, with loads of sugar.

Tom dug out - guess what - his cricket ball, and since I instinctively jumped up too (for whatever reason I don't know - obedience? Loyalty to Tom?), the school teacher beckoned to me, and we went out and threw the ball back and forth.

I drew quite a crowd of gawking men, and a few girls in the distance. Come to think of it, I'd never seen a woman play in a cricket game in India.

When we finally left, my camel took the lead again, racing along as fast as necessary to keep in the front. I had no idea where we were going, as there was no obvious trail, but it didn't matter; Kaloo seemed to know. We floated over sand tracks, with the occasional prickly acacia tree on the horizon, and a lonely goat-herder with a small herd here and there. Our group chatted and laughed as we paced along, English for us tourists and Hindi for the camel drivers. We talked to each other as if we understood the language, using gestures for emphasis. They seemed such an easy-going, happy lot.

Our Head Camel Driver, riding behind James, beckoned Dave and me back to him. Barkat reined in our Kaloo (which I am sure he was not pleased with) and rode beside them. Head Camel Driver spoke in Hindi and gestured to me and Dave. It was obvious he wanted us to sing. Dave and James and I blew through a few songs, sometimes on key, sometimes not, and they got a big kick out of it. I like listening to the camel drivers singing. They have beautiful voices.

We pulled up to a mud-and-stick shelter for lunch at noon. It was hotter today than yesterday, although a breeze picked up which felt good in the shade of the building.

Tom and Dave broke out the chess board. James felt better so he joined in. I felt absolutely wonderful, but everyone else seemed wiped out. The other four laid down in the shade on mattresses the drivers laid out. Michelle's husband Dave isn't feeling well, Michelle is iffy, Malcolm is still awfully sore from riding, and Anneli's butt is sore from riding.

We sat and relaxed and waited for lunch. We all tortured ourselves talking about the good Indian food that we'd had (and for me, everything I had eaten in this country was delicious), and the first thing we'd do and eat when we got home. Most of us were on extended travels; I was nearing three months.

For me, I said, first thing I will do is run onto my green lawn and wallow about in the grass, then soak in a long hot bubble bath, then sit down to a big hot American meal of meat and potatoes. And I'll probably get deathly ill from it too, being so used to veggie dishes and Indian spices!

Danesh called Anneli and me inside the hut-cum-kitchen for a Rajasthan desert cooking lesson. He sent Anneli out for veggies, and he instructed me on how to mix the spices together. Then Head Cook had me put the pot on the fire, feed the fire with the right amount of wood, pour in the oil and heat it up, and pour the spices in, add a dash of water and cook the spices, making them pop and crack, and stirring it just so.

Anneli came back inside with veggies, and they had her throw in onions, cauliflower and cabbage, while I stirred and stirred. And stirred some more.

Danesh said, "You are strong horse woman. Use your muscles to stir." My arm did get tired, stirring food for 12 people in a big pot! Danesh had me sample it, and then he sampled it, and then Head Cook sampled it, and we all deemed it was ready.

Head Cook pulled it off the fire, and Anneli and I retired

from the hot kitchen. It was hard work, slaving over a hot stove in the hot desert in the middle of a hot day – and it's winter! We got just a little taste of what the Indian women do, day in and day out.

The boys played their chess, I wrote in my journal (Danesh said, "Always writing!"), the others dozed, and finally lunch arrived at 2 PM – our good, spicy veggies, rotis, and rice, followed by everyone's not-so-favorite, sugar with chai. It's been very difficult for me to choke hot sugar-laden chai down, especially on a hot day.

I told Danesh I wanted a group picture, including the camel drivers, and Danesh was so enthused about it, he took over organizing it just before we mounted up and rode away. He arranged the camels symmetrically, and the drivers, then fit "the tourists" in, and we all took turns running out with cameras to get a group picture.

We mounted up and jogged off, serenaded by our camel drivers – which resembled a pack of howling coyotes. I serenaded my own boy Barkat, and he really listened as I sang.

Our Head Camel Driver rode again with James this afternoon, and he pulled up beside Kaloo and gestured to James and me and said, "Sing," in Hindi.

Now, I really have zero singing talent, but nobody I was traveling with knew that, and the camel drivers thought I was ever so talented. Or perhaps I was the funniest thing they'd ever heard. Either way, it was fun for everybody. James and I belted out some song which, as usual, cracked them up.

Kaloo kept the lead again and refused to let anyone pass us, and we actually raced James and the Head Camel Driver, and while he "hupp"ed and whipped his camel, Kaloo sprinted on by and left them in the desert dust!

We stopped at another Muslim family hut, where the family was all outside working on millet. I took a turn beating the millet with the big stick, and the women all laughed when the stick uncontrollably flew backwards out of my hand, and the woman out there with me jumped back so as not to get hit. The beating of the millet was much harder than it looked. The women had a natural rhythm, and I was completely uncoordinated.

One woman kept her face veiled because she was married and we were strangers. One older woman walked up later, with one boob hanging out but with her face totally veiled.

We left there and jogged onward, Kaloo far in the lead. Riding a camel is so smooth and comfortable, I could have dozed off in the saddle. I could picture myself being a cowboy on cattle drives back in the 1800s, living on a horse for months at a time.

Barkat sang one song again and again, and I repeated some verse after him and he laughed.

We came upon our dunes from the first night, having ridden in a big circle, where we'd camp again tonight, and we rode up on some girls out gathering wood.

Barkat told me in Hindi to sing along with him, and when he reached the verse I knew I belted it out with him. The girls and Barkat and I all busted up, and I said, "Namaste!" and folded my hands and nodded. They repeated it and giggled. That's a Nepali greeting, but they knew what I was saying.

We dismounted in the sunset, and the camel drivers unloaded us and the camel gear on the dunes. We sat around while the sun dropped below the horizon, and when the group of girls carrying bundles of sticks on their heads appeared in silhouette on the crest of the dune with the red sky at their backs, we all scrambled like delirious tourists to get pictures of them.

We had the two camel drivers still in the dunes in stitches at our predictable silliness, and they yelled out to the girls to stop and pose, and they were giggling too.

Tom pulled out his radio and let Malcolm have a listen. Malcolm felt like he had a fever and was already under two blankets. We all listened to the Hindi radio, and talked, until our jeep drove up to the dunes. Up walked Danesh's family, including the girl from the Jaisalmer guest house and their father.

Only Tom, Dave, James, and I were up for dinner so we

piled in the jeep with the family and rode to the hut by the schoolhouse. There we met the next three people leaving on tomorrow's trek.

Tom was ecstatic because Bill was another Englishman. I bet the first words out of their mouths were "Cricket!"

We were expecting Danesh's dal bhat, but we had the same old veggie and rice meal, although there wasn't as much hot chili this time. In other words, I think Head Cook re-cooked (i.e. corrected) the spices I'd concocted at lunch.

After an oh-so-not-refreshing cup o' sugar with chai, Danesh drove us back to the dunes where the musicians awaited us. I joined the circle for a while and listened to a few flute songs and a few jaw harp songs, then crawled under my blanket and drifted off...

<> <> <> <> <>

Day 4

I was again the first awake, just as the thin red line was stealing along the horizon. I crept off to wee then walked around on the dunes until my bare feet were numb – the temperature was refreshingly cold and the sand was frigid. The air was so clear and crisp.

I crawled back under my blanket until James got up, and we decided to walk to the hut in hopes breakfast would be ready. We met Danesh halfway, going to wake up and fetch the others, and they all made it to the hut before breakfast was served. So much for being early birds.

We had porridge first, toast second, jam third, and sugar chai last. Yuck! I could never get used to their sugary tea.

I went and played a little cricket with Tom, Bill, and Dave and an Indian (I still do not understand this game), then we were ready to leave at 10 AM. We said bye to Dave and Tom, Tom looking unhappy with goodbyes, especially since he's been traveling with James for four months. Tom and Dave stayed to hang out with Danesh a few more days.

We six climbed in the jeep with Danesh's family for a ride to Jodhpur, with Guyatri the sister, Papu the younger brother, the father, the driver, and a friend of the family. Michelle tried to hug Danesh but he jumped back, embarrassed and appalled, and quickly bowed Namaste; because of his Brahmin caste we weren't allowed to touch him like that.

We promised to send pictures and thanked him for a great time, and waved bye to the boys. Danesh stood and waved the longest – I think he really enjoyed our group.

We stopped after about two hours in the jeep at a school house where Paw knew the people. They called us all up for tea in the middle of class. The children all sat politely in straight rows, staring and smiling at us. We got sweet tea, then curd to drink.

Paw asked if they would all go out in the sun for a school picture. The teacher gave the word and the kids charged out, hollering and making a party out of it. I motioned some kids around into position, and soon they were lined up, some kneeling and some sitting, all in good order and being patient.

One little boy wouldn't come - Guyatri said he had polio or something, so we insisted he be carried to the picture. She interpreted for us. He was moved into the picture lineup (he looked happy to be a part of it), and Anneli, Michelle, and I all took pictures. When we finished and said, "OK," the kids all broke into a cheer and clapped and ran back to their seats. Paw told us to *please* send pictures. I hope to send a whole boodle to them.

We continued on toward Jodhpur, and two hours later we stopped at a small village to buy snacks, because we still had "an hour" before Jodhpur. We were mobbed by kids, "Hello one pen. One school pen. Hello one pen. One pen!" and a woman begged for money and food. Even Guyatri said they annoyed her.

As soon as we started reaching the traffic and exhaust fumes in the outskirts of Jodhpur, I immediately felt it in my throat, and my nose was already clogging up. What a contrast to the clean air of the desert. We got into hassle central of Jodhpur at 2:30. We all groaned. Already, our desert camel adventure in the wilds of Rajasthan was a distant memory.

I wonder if Kaloo is still racing at the front of his pack.

TRANSPORTATION: BUSES AND TRAINS

Because *of course* we decided we were tough enough to travel by unreserved second class on the long distance train from Bombay (now known as Mumbai) to Cochin (now known as Kochi), a distance of 889 miles. That's because we were Budget Backpackers, budget being the key element of our travel style, and unreserved second class fitting our budgets. (And first class was full anyway, so even if we had not been so principled, we had no other option.)

Even though we had all read about what traveling in the second-class train compartments would be like (i.e., nightmare), it was part of the accepted budget travel religion that there would be some particular suffering along the way, a form of budget travel penance, if you will, which would eventually please the Travel Gods and give you points toward your eventual good travel luck. Besides, the *Lonely Planet* made it sound like such a challenge, one that seasoned budget backpackers should be up to. And surely it couldn't be that bad, right?

And so we took that second class train, for 889 miles, and we suffered. There were a precious couple of brilliant, outstanding moments in there, and we would be rewarded by arriving in Cochin, for Christmas Eve... but oh lordy, did we suffer on the way.

And first we had to survive Indian buses before boarding the trains.

< > < > < > < > < >

December 23

I was traveling with James at the time. Bearded, quiet, calm James was an easy travel partner, seemingly able to handle anything with serenity, a valued trait in always-turbulent India. (Months later he wrote me from an ashram that he'd joined in India - he'd seen the light! and was in a blissful state!, he told me, with lots of exclamation points at the ends of all his sentences.)

James was part of the group on our terrific four-day camel trek in the Rajasthan desert together; and afterwards, James and I both decided to head way down south - not to the popular traveler's destination of Goa, which was packed during Christmas, but much further to Cochin, on the Malabar coast of the Arabian Sea, moving me closer to Madras (now Chennai), my ultimate destination to visit my Indian friends in January. I was glad he decided to accompany me.

The journey started with one of those rather unpleasant overnight bus rides, from Udaipur To Ahmedabad, aboard one of the godawful dreaded Video Buses. Whether you liked it or not, and whether or not the bus ticket salesman assures you there will absolutely be no video on the bus (as he bobs his head in that famous Indian bob that truly means yes or no, in full agreement with your vehemence), there will indeed be a horrid video running the entire ride, a Hindi movie, at top volume, so loud you wouldn't be able to understand it even if you did speak Hindi and even if it were an Oscar-winner. Ear plugs are your best friend on these video buses. Which I'd lost by this leg of my journey.

At first I thought we'd lucked out. The video wasn't that long or that loud, but it was compensated for by the bus itself, which was so bumpy and DEAFENING. The way the windows were rattling, it sounded like I was lying in a foxhole directly between two front lines of fire in battle.

I thought, my head is rattling just like that, on this bumpy-ass road. My brains are going to shake loose from my skull. My teeth are going to fall out. One couldn't really even doze, because there was no rhythm to the rattling noise; and it was difficult to keep your balance, even in the reclining seats, with all the potholes the driver slammed into and/or tried to dodge around. Or maybe he was trying to hit them, because there were an awful lot of terrible jarring bumps, some so severe I was afraid the bus would shatter.

Then while trying to doze, suddenly a hand grabbed my left forearm under my shawl and pushed down hard, like they were trying to pump water from my stomach or perform CPR on me. In fact, the hand was likely trying to find and grab and squeeze my boob. What the hell?

I was too groggy to retaliate but I got my eyes open to see it was the man right across the aisle from me - who, when I stared at him, sat very straight in his seat looking wide-eyed straight ahead - which was a dead guilty giveaway, when everybody else on the bus was reclining and sleeping.

I dozed off again, and at the next stop, the jackass did it again! Seriously? Did he have nothing better to do!? This time he grabbed my upper arm through my shawl – groping higher for my boob, since he knew it had to be up in there somewhere, but he missed again. I tried to slug him, but it only came out as a thump on his arm because I couldn't get my arm untangled from the shawl.

But I did thunder, "KEEP YOUR GODDAMN HANDS OFF ME!" Again he sat up looking straight ahead, deer-in-the-headlights-frozen, which was just as well screaming that he was the culprit. If he hadn't done anything, he'd have looked at me like I was nuts, as everybody else around me was doing. James asked if I wanted to trade seats, so I could sit by the window out of reach, but I bellowed, in the guilty man's direction, "NO, NOT UNLESS THIS JACKASS TRIES IT AGAIN!"

So much for sleep; so much for peace on this bus. The man didn't touch me again, but then I didn't doze off again, and I had my left arm uncovered and ready to slug. I sure hoped the trains would be better. Surely they could not be any worse than this, no matter what rumors we'd heard.

< > < > < > < > < >

We arrived at the Ahmedabad bus station at 4:15 AM. I had to pee badly, but do you think there's a woman's bathroom anywhere around? Of course not. There's no men's bathroom either, which is no problem because they just peed anywhere and everywhere, against or on anything they felt like. James stood guard while I ran around behind a bus in the dark and let go on the cement.

We caught a rickshaw (it goes without saying, bargaining down to half of the first price) to the train station, and there we found we could hop right onto the 5 AM train to Bombay, arriving there at 1:30 PM, and catch the 3:30 PM train, Express Superfast to Cochin, arriving there around 7 AM Christmas Eve.

We were a bit elated, since we thought we might still be sitting on a train on Christmas Day. It sounded too good to be true.

But wait: the only catch was, we had to ride on the dreaded second class unreserved cars because no first class was available. Oh, God. Well, we had to do it. We could do this. Because we were Budget Backpackers.

We hopped right on the 5 AM train to Bombay, and found seats with no problem. If this was the worst second class unreserved could throw at us, well heck, bring it on! This was so much better than that dreadful bus ride! I dozed in my seat for an hour - rather soundly it seemed, because by the time I woke up, our train car had suddenly filled up, and I didn't remember us stopping.

Now there seemed to be another 30 people getting on at every stop. It was standing room only now. James and I now had only one seat between us, and we kept switching off.

It got miserably hot after the sun rose, but I didn't want to give anyone ideas I was stripping by pulling off my sweatshirt, even though I had a T-shirt on underneath. I finally couldn't take it anymore and had to peel it off once James gave me the seat again. My underwear and sweats were already stuck to my skin like glue from the stuffy overnight bus ride (Indians seemed to not like fresh air; they liked to keep the bus windows clamped shut); I had a bad and painful cough, and I felt crumpled like I do when I don't get enough sleep.

But on the whole, this second class unreserved train ride was not too bad. It was doable. Maybe we could pull this whole trip off without too much misery!

< > < > < > < > < >

We pulled into Bombay Central Train Station at 1 PM, and after being pointed to the TC office, whatever that is, the nice, friendly, helpful, English-speaking Indian man there told us we had to catch our train from Victoria Terminus Station, and even how much to pay the taxi to get there.

Once at Victoria Terminus, we found out that an hour before departure on platform 12 we could try for any remaining spots on the first-class reserved cars. We were not wimps or anything, but, you know, if first class had seats available, it was a sign that we should take advantage of them.

We whiled away the time at a questionable cafeteria, then went out to the train platform at 2:30, where we were stunned by an absolute boggling mass of humanity with all their luggage, a chaotic cacophony whirling together in a monster dervish.

To our consternation, we found that it was an absolutely full train, no chance at all for any first class reserved seats. Oh, God, we were indeed going to be riding a 15-hour, unreserved, second-class overnight train, and this astounding mass of humanity was going to be riding crammed in right beside us. What an experience this was going be.

One man offered to find us two seats on a second-class car, for 70 rupees each. "70 rupees!" I said. "No way!" In my concrete

Budget Travel mind, this was a whole two American dollars! Completely unacceptable!

Next guy offered to find us seats for 20 rupees each, and we agreed, sending him off to look. Sure enough, he gestured to us from the door of a carriage and led us to: one entire top 'bunk,' (i.e. the luggage rack above a bench seat) for James and me and our backpacks; and despite the 3,752 people on this one car, once we crawled up there, nobody even tried to make us move, not that we were going to budge, not even with a lit stick of dynamite beneath our butts.

Well... things could be worse, I thought... and they really were, when I looked around me. People sat on the floors, on laps, on laps on the floors, five to a bench made for three, people in their laps, two to a single seat; it was hot, noisy, my head already hurt, and we were going to be perched up here for 15 hours. Compared to everybody else, though, we were in the lap of luxury, even if we couldn't completely sit up straight on our luggage rack without cracking our heads. We could at least sprawl over our bags and each other in somewhat comfortable various positions.

We could not, however, see outside at all. Each cubbyhole had windows at eye level with the people on the benches, but we had nothing but train car walls and ceiling around us. That was a little disconcerting, but it (so far) didn't feel too terribly claustrophobic, if I didn't think about it.

Some of the people below us on the benches (there were at least 10 of them), as well as the four people and their bags crammed onto the luggage rack across from us, eyed us with what I figured had to be jealousy at our roomy perch.

I laughed and told James, "If I had known I'd be spending Christmas like this, I'd have stayed at home!" If my mom could see me now! I'm not particularly religious, but my mantra to get me through this, was Cochin: Christmas Eve service in a church.

< > < > < > < > < >

Chaos on board a typical Indian second-class unreserved train car:

At one station stop, a man boarded with apples and nearly started a riot on the car, as he jostled and stumbled and tripped his way through people sprawled and packed in the aisle. The whole car of passengers started screaming, the apple man screamed and gestured and shoved apples at people and grabbed them back. He sliced off bites, stuffed some in his mouth while yelling, handed some slices out, grabbed some back. I couldn't figure out what everyone was so hysterical about. I mean, either you want apples or you don't.

I thought the apple man was going to start slashing with his knife, as he was about to go off on a Speed Wobble. Never had I seen such excitement, such madness, over apples. He looked up at us on our luggage rack, locking eyes with mine, while stabbing the air with apples and his knife, and with wide eyes I shook my head, no, no no, no way, go away, I'm afraid of you and your apples.

At every train stop, there was a continuous parade of merchants who boarded our car, and elbowed their way up and down the crowded aisle, selling tea, food, trinkets.

While rolling along, one man on the bench below us suddenly got a burr under his butt and started screaming and punching the guy across from us on the luggage rack, who was egging him on; and he gestured at us a few times. They must have been arguing over our cushy lodgings, but fight or no fight on a stuffy train car with 3,000 people, no way was I budging.

Perhaps one of those men was standing up for our honor, but I couldn't figure out who or what exactly was going on, and while I shrank from swinging fists, I fiercely threw the Stink Eye about, as in, Don't even THINK about squeezing up here with us or kicking us out. We paid the same as you! Or, as foreigners, probably more!

Finally around 9:30 PM as darkness set in, people started settling down a bit, like a flock of birds getting ready to hunker down in their trees for the night; and the bench men quit eying our 'roomy' rack and more or less left us alone.

Two nice men across from us, one above on their jammed luggage rack with four people and luggage, and one below jammed in with five other people on that bench, shared their dinner with us - jam and bread, a boiled egg, and roti. We were so grateful, as in a poor execution of meal planning, James and I had nothing but stale crackers and water between us.

It had been hot during the day, but at least our compartment kicked the fans on, which circulated the oven-like air and made it bearable. It never got cold during the night, and in fact when we stopped at the multitude of stations along the way, it got rather warm in the car, without the 'fresh' air barely creeping through the small windows below us.

James and I tried and tried to get comfortable and doze. Our human bodies weren't made to sleep sitting up on hard straight Indian second-class train car luggage rack "seats."

Finally James arranged some combination of our bags to lay on, and we got a little bit of sleep.

< > < > < > < > < >

December 24

I came to around 6 AM having to pee mightily, but, thinking of the terrific commotion I'd set off, having to climb down on top of everybody, most of whom were still dozing, and crawl over every person in our little cubby hole, and a thousand more standing and sleeping people in the aisles to the bathroom at the end of the car, I thought I'd just hold it until we got off the train in Cochin at 7 AM.

James and I started talking with the man below us who spoke a wee bit of English, and he seemed to be telling us we were in Karnataka... which is only some 403 miles from Bombay...with 486 more miles to go until Cochin...and the realization slowly dawned on us that we'd get to Cochin

TOMORROW morning, 7 AM.

Oh. My. God. James and I looked at each other with the stupidest, most shocked and numbed expressions – 24 MORE HOURS on this train…!!

What could we do but start laughing! Ohmigod – Christmas Eve not in a church but in this hot stuffy mad Indian Zoo cage slowly rolling along a countryside I couldn't see!

We literally sat, unable to speak for a while – we could only look at each other dumbly and laugh! And stare down the packed train car, and laugh! Oh, God.

I had been waiting to pee until we got off in Cochin, but seeing as Cochin was 24 hours away, I really had to go. I put my shoes on (you take them off if you're up top), said Excuse me, sorry, excuse me, and climbed down from our perch trying not to step on top of the people on the bench below us, and I fought my way to the bathroom, searching for places to put my feet, as every single inch of floor space was sat or stood upon.

I had to wait in line, and right when my turn came, and finally I shoved my way into the loo, wouldn't you know, just as I squatted over the hole in the floor, of course we pulled into a station.

And of course there was no window cover, so people could see me squatting. Good grief! I couldn't just stay there like a naked deer caught in headlights of a thousand gawkers (not to mention crapping on the train tracks in the station), so I unsquatted, shoved the bathroom door open in disgust (and disappointment and discomfort), fought my way through the people pouring off the train, rammed my way through the people getting on and looking for a seat, shoved into our cubby and clambered back up to my perch and took my shoes off. James said, "Well that was quick."

I said, "I didn't get to go! There was a window and I was on full display! I have to go back when the train starts moving!"

When the train pulled out from the station fifteen minutes later, I grabbed my toothbrush and water bottle, put my shoes back on, and started my long journey again, excusing myself, shouldering and shoving my way back to the bathroom, and waiting in line. Once I got in there I took my time!

Somewhat emptied and cleaned and 'refreshed', I crawled and squeezed through the mass of bodies back to our perch and climbed up and sat, still (so far) in fairly good humor despite another 24 hours of this misery ahead.

The man below gave me an egg and jam and bread for breakfast, and we rolled on slowly through India on the decidedly NOT Express Superfast train to Cochin...

It started getting hot and humid and sticky, despite the fans. The man below told James in his broken English to ask for a sleeper car at a station. I'm sure, even in his own discomfort, that dear man was thinking more of our discomfort. Or maybe he was still dreaming about sprawling in our vacated roomy luggage rack.

I dozed a while, then sat up after I woke up drenched in sweat, my heart pounding, just as if I'd been laying in a hot sun.

The train stopped for 'lunch' at a station around 1 PM, and from my perch, I pointed out the window below what I wanted from vendors, and the Nice Man told me the Indian prices, and paid the money I handed him to the vendor out the window, and collected the change and handed that back to me with our food.

James jumped off the train at this station to ask at the ticket counter about a second-class sleeper car, but none were available. "Maybe at the next station," he said.

A vendor woman came through our car with bananas, but she didn't create any uproar like the apple man did. She handed James a bunch of eight stubby bananas. The Nice Man took them and inspected them carefully. "Five rupees," he proclaimed, making sure we got the local Indian price. We handed down five rupees.

I dozed off after I ate again; in the sweltering box of madness my resilience began to wane, and despair was starting to creep into my fortitude-waning travel bones, and I had trouble fighting off images of Christmas Eve at home. Really, now, why was I even here in India over the holidays? What was I thinking?

I woke up sweating again at a train stop, and James was gone; and when the train pulled out, he didn't return! He was either in another train car or he had been left behind in the station...and to keep total despair from submerging me I refused to believe he might've missed the train. I would've just sat there and cried. I didn't even know what the hell I would do if he had missed the train... get off at the next stop with all our stuff, and wait for him and the next train? Go on another 24 hrs to Cochin in this horrid car by myself with our bags, and get off there and wait for him? I simply could not think about it. He'd be back in this car at the next stop, or the next. He had to be.

Next station stop I waited patiently, and partly in a daze, because it was too hot to do anything else, and James popped his head around the corner, "Let's go. I got us two sleepers!"

Oh YES!!!! Hallelujah! I threw my shoes on, jumped down, tossed James his pack, threw my packs on, and said "Bye!"

We were swallowed in a loud chorus of "BYE!"s, more from happiness our seats were being vacated then from any friendly warmth, except for the Nice Man who smiled and nodded at us. I think he was a Saint sent to our train car and compartment specifically to watch over us.

I followed James, elbowing and forcing our way off the crowded train car through the cascade of people getting on and off, and we dashed alongside the train looking for car S-6, as the train started to pull away, moving towards us.

But no sireee, we weren't getting left behind! We reached our car and grabbed hold and swung on (the locals are pros at this), and walked down the aisle of the car (which was not jam-packed with people), only to find people sitting in our seats in a compartment. But they said they were getting off at the next stop. James sat in a vacant seat in the aisle, and I left my pack with him and went and stood in the path by the two open doors to the outside, the ground rushing by (at Superfast Express putt-putt speed). People hung off the doors, and some guys climbed from car to car on the roof of the moving train. One probably didn't need train tickets for that! The wind felt so good, and I felt such a release from the Unreserved Zoo car. I wondered if I really would've survived another night on that luggage rack.

Next stop we got our seats, and sat by two open windows as the train chugged on past the sunset. Perhaps it was coincidence, or a beautiful gift that our windows faced west and played out the most spectacular sunset I'd ever seen.

A pond we passed enhance the brilliant colors and small mountains. I thought, wow, this is a good sign, this must be another one of my Christmas presents - sitting in this car in my own seat and watching the sunset out a window I could actually look and breathe fresh air out of.

I didn't write in my journal, like I needed to do. I just sat transfixed, gazing at the sunset. A brilliant shade of red burned before fading to darkness.

And then everything was dark, as we had no lights in our car, but it didn't matter. We had seats to ourselves!

The group of eight boys sitting in our compartment belonged to some Hindu cult that wore black and no shoes and fasted for 41 days. They started talking to us, and leaning closer and closer and giving us the third degree.

They were just polite and curious, but what with the pitch dark and their dark clothes, I couldn't see a thing and I didn't trust them one bit.

But then their sadhu gathered them together under his wings and they got off at the next stop. Now there were just four of us in our four-bench compartment, each with a sleeping bench to ourselves! The lap of luxury! Who needed a first-class train ticket in India!

I just sat, enjoying the drastic improvement in the travel conditions (we had one tense moment when the ticket checker didn't seem to want to accept our tickets, but in the end he did), enjoying the pleasant sound and motion of the train, enjoying the breeze blowing on me from the open window right at my face, humming Christmas tunes to myself in the dark, thinking, maybe Christmas in India isn't so bad after all, if I make it to the

St. Francis church service tomorrow morning.

But I still couldn't let myself think of what everyone was doing at home...

< > < > < > < > < >

December 25

Despite having to get up once for the loo (which was easy, since I didn't have to crawl over and step on 3,500 people), and waking up once with a coughing fit, it was one of my best sleeps ever on the rhythmic, rolling train through the Indian countryside.

I woke up at 6 AM. James poked his head out of his sleeping bag from his bench across from me. "Merry Christmas," I said. "Merry Christmas," he said.

"Happy Christmas!" said one of the Hindus.

I opened the window - because I could! - to scents of palm tree plantations and mist and a warm morning.

7 AM passed, and we hadn't gotten to Ernakulam yet. I started to get a little anxious – I was this close, 10 kilometers away – I just couldn't miss church service after all of this.

Finally around 8 AM we arrived at the Ernakulam Junction station and got off the train. Even on Christmas day, the tuk tuk drivers wanted to rip us off. So, being the strictly principled Budget Travelers that we were, we brushed off the drivers and walked to the ferry terminal, even though time was ticking down. It was definitely warmer and more humid here.

Wanting the Cochin ferry, we waited and waited for a ticket man to show up, until some man walking by said to us lonely and forlorn backpackers, "No ferries today." No ferries on Christmas!

So we tried for a bus, one of which we fortunately caught right away, just outside the ferry stop, and after a short ride we got off at the Cochin bus stop, just a few blocks from the church.

We passed the Elite Hotel which looked all closed up; we

banged on a door, and from the inside a man told us to try the Princess Hotel down the street. We took a shabby, mosquito-infested double room in the Princess for a very reasonable amount of rupees, threw our packs down, and raced to St. Francis Church.

We walked in during the last part of the service; just in time for communion. I was so hot and dirty and sticky, and wearing a hot pink T-shirt, but I didn't care.

Now, as I said, I'm not really particularly religious, and neither was James, but after the constant stress and bombardment of traveling in Hindu India, I was so happy to be there in a familiar culture that gave me just a taste of home Christmas with family, I could've cried, and I almost did!

A Christmas tree (though not a real pine Christmas tree) decorated with lights adorned the front of the church near the pulpit, the service was in English, it was the best bread and wine I'd ever had, and as people walked out of church at the end of the service, the organist played Silent Night – my first and only Christmas carol this year... only he stopped in the middle of the second verse, closed up the organ and walked out while we still sat in the pews.

CHAPTER 3:
ZIMBABWE, 1995

I might die today

Why Zimbabwe?

Six years earlier, I'd met South African Janet on a ski-lift ride up to Ehrenbreitstein Fortress, our youth hostel castle for the night in Koblenz, Germany. We hit it off, and traveled together for a few days in Germany. Good times. We stayed in touch afterwards over the years, and she invited me to use her home as a base if I ever decided to visit southern Africa.

And so, six years later, I went to southern Africa.

I arrived in Johannesburg and stayed with Janet and her husband Anthony a few days, before traveling solo around South Africa, and then taking off on a backpacker's bus trip through Namibia, Botswana, and Zimbabwe.

At Victoria Falls, I met back up with Janet and Anthony and their cousin Vicki for more adventures in Zimbabwe: rafting the Zambezi river at Victoria Falls, and canoeing the Zambezi river below Kariba dam.

RAFTING THE MIGHTY ZAMBEZI RIVER

What the hell, I had said. I'll just do it. I didn't really want to, but I agreed to go white-water rafting with my South African friends down the Zambezi river in Victoria Falls, Zimbabwe.

The Zambezi is the fourth-longest river in Africa. With headwaters in a triangle junction of Zambia, Democratic Republic of the Congo (formerly Zaire), and Angola, it reaches Zimbabwe, where it plunges over the famous Victoria Falls (where the adventure rafting begins), and flows 200 miles down to the Kariba dam, where it's corralled and tamed for power generation.

On top, we'd looked across the gorge at the Mosi-oa-Tunya, or "Thundering Smoke" (in the Lozi language), or the Shungu Namutitima, or "Boiling Water" (in the Tonga language), as one of the largest waterfalls in the world plunged 354 feet down and over a mile wide, off the Zambia plateau. We could feel the spray - and the power - from Victoria falls. It was most certainly thundering and boiling beneath. We'd be climbing into our rafts in the bottom of the gorge below these falls.

Early in the morning, the four of us headed to the Makasa Sun Hotel for our gathering and briefing on our Date With Destiny.

I volunteered to be a paddler...but that was before one river guide told us that those in the paddle boats flipped more often.

Well, what the hell, I told myself. I remembered my sister-in-law Barbara riding the rapids on a river in Colorado, and saying "When the guide yelled, 'PADDLE!' I just paddled!" If she, a 55-year-old school teacher who claimed to have done nothing more daring than downhill ski on bunny slopes could white-water raft, surely I, who climbed mountains and rode crazy horses and traveled around the world, could be brave for just a few hours of one day and paddle a raft down a white-water river also.

I signed the indemnity paper...but that was before the "What to do in case of..." speech. When the speaking guide got to the part about the Hole, it all suddenly came back to me – the dreaded HOLE, the time I got caught in a HOLE on a somewhat tame river in Texas and almost drowned. I vividly felt again the sudden slam into the water with no air, no escape from the HOLE, tumbling under torrents of water, no sense of direction, panic, no air, lungs bursting, tumbling, *no escape,* NO MORE AIR.

My heart pounded even as he spoke.

"So...uh...what *do* you do if you get caught in one?" I asked him.

He laughed. "Panic!"

That was not funny. Nobody else laughed. He never gave an answer.

We went through the rest of the What Ifs, such as, What If you got your foot caught under a boulder under the water, or What If you smashed your head even while wearing a helmet and a life vest and you were knocked unconscious under water, none of which were answered reassuringly, and none of which we would remember anyway when it came to split-second events unfolding in a ferocious river crashing around slow-motion human reactions. I was not feeling good about any of this.

There were something like 130 people in our group that would fill 16 rafts - three hold-on rafts where the guide paddled and everyone else held on, and the rest were boats full of paddlers - the paddle boats that tend to flip more often - that I'd unthinkingly volunteered to ride in.

My South African friend Vicki was having her doubts. I was beyond having doubts and was saying my prayers. I'd rather be bungi jumping off the bridge over the Zambezi river, and that was saying a lot, because I sure didn't want to do that either. (Afterwards, I did bungi jump off the bridge over the Zambezi river...but that's another tale.)

We were split into groups of seven, and my group was assigned a guide, Warren; and we began the slow hiking descent to the Zambezi to our awaiting boats.

There was some noise in the distance, a steady breeze or something that steadily grew in intensity as we walked. My stomach tightened when I realized it was the Zambezi river itself making that din, which sounded more and more like an escalating storm, the closer we got.

We picked up life jackets and helmets on the way, and continued down the slippery trail, step by step, marching closer to our doom. There was a lot of silence from our big group, which became thick and heavy as the roar of the water became louder and oppressive.

"I feel like I'm marching into Vietnam," one guy tittered nervously. Nobody laughed at that.

Wearing our battle gear - jackets and helmets - and carrying our river weapons - our paddles – we sweated, from the steamy tropical humidity and from nervousness. For most people there, it was the first time to raft such a ferocious river. They didn't know exactly what to expect, though we all knew this was something big, something exciting, something where we would not be in control.

I *knew* what was out there. I couldn't get the HOLE out of my head, and the sensations that went with the word. My heart pounded from the exertion of climbing down to the river, and with fear. Wasn't this supposed to be fun? My steps became more sluggish and leaden the closer I got to the river. I had a *bad* feeling about this.

I guess I could've turned back...but I didn't. The troops

were marching forward; I had to go with them.

We got down to our boats. The roar of the unseen rapids were conspicuous: *fierce.* Warren put my group into our positions in our paddle boat (my friends Anthony, Janet, another man, and me on the left; a boy, a girl, Vicki, and Warren on the right) and we started practicing responding to Warren's commands.

To go left, the left side paddled backward and the right side paddled forward; to go right, the opposite. I knew this was crucial. Back goes left, forward goes right, I memorized. Just four life-and-death words to remember. *Sure, easy,* you people in your armchairs are saying, but you try this when your heart is stuck in your throat and the ravenous rapids are roaring a hundred yards away around the bend and you know you might die today.

Warren commanded: "OK – forward!" We pounded our paddles into the water. Crack crack – we kept hitting each other. "Get a rhythm!" Finally we got one, and the 16-foot inflatable moved forward smoothly.

"LEFT! Quickly!" Our minds froze; we all just reacted - in eight different ways. *Back left!* I told myself, and found myself paddling forward. We churned the water mightily, and our boat remained in its position and didn't turn at all.

Warren sat back in despair...though the boy did not *know* what real despair was compared to the sinking pit of dread I was feeling in my stomach.

"Guys, you're going to *have* to get this down before we start. It's critical that you respond correctly to my commands, instantly." Or what, I thought, death? Fall out in a HOLE and drown?! A wave of what was a prelude to hysteria raced through me and I bit my tongue. *Breathe,* I told myself, *keep breathing.*

Warren went over it again. We practiced paddling. I was thinking, this could seriously be life or death, so I better get this down. Somebody remind me, why the hell was I doing this?

I got my responses down – left back, right forward. "Forward!" (We paddled forward.) "Left!" (Backpaddle.) "Forward!" (Forward.) "Hard right! HardRight!" (Dig in hard forward.) "Left left!" (Hard back.) "Forward." (Forward)...

We were getting it down past our ears, hopefully into our subconscious, down to the response nerves in our bodies. In this sheltered, still water we were getting it, anyway. We paddled up to the video cameraman, executed some of Warren's commands, then ceremoniously threw ourselves into the water, as if this were the Happiest and Funnest Place On Earth. *And,* I prayed, *may this be the only time today that I hit the water.*

Then...the time had arrived to stride into battle. We climbed back into our boat into our positions, and floated closer to the first rapid, #4, Morning Glory, the rumble of the river growing ever more menacing. My heart was pounding so hard throughout my body, my fingertips sent little tremors into the paddle I was clenching.

We held our position near the bank as we waited for the whole group of boats to be ready. The river thundered steadily now, and I could just see the top of the rapid. Warren started telling us how to negotiate this one but my ears were pounding so hard with rushing blood and adrenaline that I couldn't remember anything he'd just said.

We laughed, and joked, putting on a brave face in the face of death. There perhaps wasn't great danger of drowning (although a couple of deaths did occur each year) – our guides were excellent (Warren had rafted this river for six months) and there were about four kayakers positioned at different spots in the rapids to pick up people thrown into the water.

But try telling my nerves that. You could figure the rafting companies didn't merrily advertise or crow about the deaths that had occurred on this river. We waited, and let most of the other rafts pass us. "I'm giving you time to relax," said Warren. Was that a joke?

"OK, here we go! Right turn!" *Oh, shit,* I thought, and threw my paddle into the water, fighting my terror with hard defiant physical expression. I hoped Nyami Nyami, the Snake-Serpent River God of the Zambezi, would be in a good mood today.

Just listen to Warren and respond, I told myself, *and for God's sake, before you hit the water TAKE A BREATH.*

"Forward!" Warren yelled, like a drill sergeant. Our raft team paddled in unison, perfect troops in perfect synchronized movement, slipping into the current, edging closer to the lip of white water.

We were upon it. The boat's nose began to dip down into it. Warren's voice became that of a frenetic World War battle general. "HARD FORWARD! GO! GO!"

I picked up his chant, yelling at Janet, yelling for me, "GO! GO!" and stabbed the Zambezi with a mighty intensity, leaning out like a pro to meet the water, as the boat began to rise and buck through a wall of boisterous crashing whiteness.

"RIGHT! FORWARD! HARD RIGHT! LEFT!" Warren yelled. My body and paddle responded; I dug for my life. I was pitched into the middle of the boat (better than out of it). I scrambled, I couldn't see a thing but spraying white; didn't know what was coming next. I reached for the side of the boat, got thrown hard into it. We were impotent humans challenging a mighty, violent river. *Folly,* my brain shot the message out, *this is lunacy. This is stupid.*

"FORWARD! GET UP! FORWARD!" Warren shouted. I sat back up, threw my paddle back into the Zambezi, fought it, defied it to pull me in (while praying it wouldn't). All around our little insignificant raft, the monstrous water swirled and boomed, a maelstrom of tossing waves and power, slamming the floating bucking raft about at its whim, toying with the eight inconsequential arrogant humans aboard a bobbing cork who sought to influence the outcome with tiny wooden sticks.

The Zambezi let us go this time. "STOP!" yelled Warren. "WOOHOO!" he yelled. Before we knew it, we were through. The look on our faces was shell shock, exhilaration. We made it through our first rapid! My heart still slammed madly – now from exertion. I was too stunned to feel any fear at the moment. I hadn't fallen out, I didn't die, I made it!

We had time to exhale and laugh and joke and regroup

before our next rapid, #5, Stairway to Heaven. Warren gave us the lowdown. "It's the highest commercial-run rapid. The drop is 16 feet." (16 feet?!)

He told us how to technically negotiate it which I immediately forgot, except for the very first step. "We MUST hit this dead center, and paddle HARD! and then..." Whatever, I forgot. That's all I could retain. My heart was still slamming at 180 bangs a minute, but now the physical exertion was gone and the fear had crept back, worse than before, pounding the adrenaline out to my fingertips. *This time, I'm going to die,* I thought.

I jammed my right foot under the center inflated cross-tube – my only anchor – and swallowed hard.

"Here we go!" *Oh, shit.* We hit the lip of the second rapid, the roar becoming deafening, and when the nose of the boat pointed down that big drop, I saw and felt a bottomless pit.

"DIG!" yelled Warren. "DIG!"

I dug, I yelled to Janet, "DIG!" She yelled "DIG!" Down, down, the nose of the raft pointed. It was like going over the brink of a roller coaster – down and impossibly more down while it left your stomach up top. I screeched in panic as our boat slid down into the HOLE and bucked back up through the wall of water that the HOLE formed.

I felt the boat go up, and up...like it was heading over backwards. "SHIT!" I screamed at the river, and stabbed at it with my paddle. I sliced through air. I sliced again and again at the air.

The raft objected to the whimsy of the white-water, bucking and folding like a piece of paper. I was thrown again, into the center of the raft. We were all hurled about, but Warren kept yelling out commands. I didn't know if he was in the human pile or if he was the only one left paddling.

I was stuck up to my knee in the middle of the boat now and couldn't move; the raft kept arching and twisting as we were stuck in the backwash of the HOLE; Warren kept yelling "DIG! DIG!" Frantically and from my sitting position, by God, I reached over the boat's side and dug into and fought the water.

I didn't remember emerging out the other side. Another rapid, safely negotiated: thrill, relief, another post-adrenaline surge. I was still in the boat's middle, stuck up to my knee.

Warren gave us a little mid-battle pep talk. "When I tell you to crouch, you do this!" (I never heard him yell crouch - I just kept paddling.)

I was still firmly stuck in the middle of the raft. Now, maybe this should have worried me, because what if the raft had flipped, and I'd been stuck with my leg in the boat like this? "I saw some of you paddling while you were sitting down in the boat!" Warren said, looking at me.

"That's because I'M STUCK!" We all laughed, letting off tension, and Warren helped extricate my leg.

We floated on down to rapid #6, the Devil's Bowl. *Oh, swell!* I thought.

Fast breathing and heartbeat still: one-third fear, one-third adrenaline, one-third excitement. Warren told us the route through the rapid. I promptly forgot it. The retention part of my brain had fallen overboard in the first rapid.

I wedged my foot under the middle cross-tube of the raft – by now the skin on top of my foot and toes was rubbing raw, but no way in hell was I not trying to anchor my foot under there for some kind of brace.

We headed in to see the Devil, brandishing our paddles and attacking it. "GO! GO!" Warren bellowed. "HARD FORWARD! GO!" Listen to Warren, attack the rapids, ride the tossing walls of water.

I yelled, I dug; the raft lurched and objected. The Zambezi roared. I was too intent to be frightened. And Nyami Nyami plucked me from the raft and pulled me in. My foot anchor was ludicrously useless. One neat bounce, and gracefully, like a swan (I like to think), I was bumped backwards off the boat, butt first, into the churning, rumbling white-water.

Instinct, this time, produced a split second reaction: I got a breath before I was unceremoniously and brusquely sucked under. I didn't panic this time (my brain was still working). *I needed more air,* but I had some air, I had time yet. And this wasn't a HOLE.

I was swished around underwater; bubbles and a different kind of gentler roaring everywhere. I detected the boat moving over me. I grabbed, floundered for the rope that I knew ran around the rim of the raft. Couldn't get it. I *had* to be so close.

But I missed it, lost the raft; and I started to feel a twinge of alarm. I needed air now, I had to have air soon - *breathe when you feel air, don't panic...*

I felt air. I gasped it in. I got air and I got the Zambezi too - I swallowed a gallon of it. I coughed half the gallon back up. My life jacket held me up, head above the river; I was through and past the rapids, was flowing downstream.

Gasping and coughing some more, I got in the float position (I remembered that valuable tidbit of preparation) and saw my trusty guide Warren and faithful paddlers coming toward me, paddling hard to pick me up before we hit the next rapid.

I was still gasping and gagging when Anthony grabbed me and hauled me back on board. I was scared, you bet, but I wasn't drowned! It wasn't nearly as bad as the Texas HOLE. I coughed up the other half of the Zambezi that I had swallowed (hopefully all the giardia and bilharzia too), in gratitude.

Rapid #7, Gulliver's Travels, next. Lots of adrenaline. This was the longest, most technical run, Warren told us. I tried to concentrate, but after the first lefts and rights and centers and all, I was lost, and ready to just go get it over with.

I'd had just enough time to get scared again, and realize I was *not* having fun. I thought, *This time, fuck the 'PADDLE! PADDLE!;' when I start to get tossed, I am going for the rope to hold on.* Janet was grabbing the rope and holding on through the rapids, and by God, I was NOT going in that damn water again, no matter what.

We paddled forward into it, Warren bawling, "HARD! GO! GO!" I lunged, I slashed, I hollered at the Zambezi and at Nyami Nyami: "NO! NO!" I was not going in again, ever.

The raft rose, fell, rose high... I slashed air. My paddle was my lifeline, my offensive sword, slashing at the enemy that wanted to take me down, take me in.

The boat got smacked by a big side wave that sent us all tumbling. I grabbed for the rope. I got slammed again and lost my grip. I grasped for the rope again, got it, and held on with a death grip. Warren was back up against the raft's side, paddling and yelling commands; I pulled myself back in position and when I got my foot jammed in securely again, I reacted to his commands. We went up another mountainous wall of water and I got slammed again, and almost bit it. I hacked back angrily at the cursed water, I stabbed viciously to Warren's "HARD RIGHT! HARD RIGHT!" My muscles protested, but I dug for my life.

Another rapid, unscathed. This time my heart must have been ramming at 220. I felt like I'd just run up Mount Everest. My chest hurt from the great gasps of oxygen I gulped. My whole being ached from the fear now racking me.

We had time to catch our breaths before #8, Midnight Diner. "If we go center, that's a Class V; it's very likely we could have our first flip. If we go right," and he said this with a disparaging tone, "it's only a Class III."

A *flip?*

Everybody: "Class V! Yea! Flip!"

A *flip?! Everybody wanted the raft to flip!?*

Me – *No fucking way.* "We go right."

We argued; I was adamant – I wanted to go right. I was not hitting the water again, especially not in a HOLE – which is what would flip the raft over in the center of this rapid. Were these people insane? Vicki was wavering, but was pressurized to vote center. I offered to get out and walk around the rapid.

Warren knew I'd jump out and swim to shore. He could see the yellow in my eyes. He even tried to find me a ride on another raft going to the right, tried to embarrass me, but I didn't give a shit. I was unabashedly scared now, and would have been paralyzed if we went for a flipped raft, and therefore quite likely to go in the water, and I'd be quite incapable of anything after that.

Warren said deprecatingly, "OK, if *she* wants to go right, we have to go right." Everyone in the boat (but my friends) sighed, so disappointed in me. *Kiss my ass,* I thought. *Damn right I am scared.* This was *not* fun for me; I wanted *out* of here.

And so, we were the only boat that went to the right. And, we were the only boat who lost their guide!

Warren started out taking this casually, since, geez, this was the pansy-ass side of the rapid, but his voice soon became frantic, barking out commands, and we paddled, as usual, for our lives. Our raft slid through twisting, gushing, gut-slamming torrents of thundering foam. The boat bucked and buckled. We were all thrown off our sides into the middle of the raft, tangling arms and bodies and paddles.

"Man overboard!" yelled Vicki; she turned to Warren, but it was he who was gone! Our fearless guide, in the water, with none of us any more capable of reading a rapid than reading Braille – *oh shit!* I saw one of Warren's hands on the outer rope, and the other hand trying to pull himself back in; I moved over (was thrown, rather) to give him a hand up. "NO! I'M FINE!" he barked over the roar. Hmm, did I detect, in all that chaos, a tenor of embarrassment from our guide?

I leaped back to my side, saw a wall of water coming at me – what do you do with no guide in the boat!? You dig! Who cares what direction – you just dig! "DIG!" I yelled.

Janet yelled back, "DIG!" and we seven amateurs pulled ourselves through the rest of the boiling rapids just as Warren flopped like a fish back into the boat. We then paddled like hell to go pick up other people from other rafts that had fallen in when their boats flipped. Warren couldn't believe he had taken a dip. I must admit to a terrible temporary smugness at that unexpected event.

Rapid #9, Commercial Suicide, was so dangerous, a Class VI, we portaged the rafts around. Thank God for some common sense. One guy in a kayak did it. It had two nasty big HOLES, one of which he disappeared under for a few seconds, before being spit out dozens of yards downstream.

We had one more rapid to ride through before lunch; but setting foot on solid ground while portaging around Commercial Suicide spelled my total white-water adventure collapse.

I did not want to get back on the water.

That was one of the hardest things I've ever done, forcing myself to climb back into that raft for one more Zambezi rapid. My fear was now so intense that I could feel my thinking and physical reactions slowing down. I had that near-nauseous feeling and a bad metallic taste in my mouth. Adrenaline wasn't going to work any more to get me through this. I knew what was next: paralytic fear and the inability to react at all. I knew me, and I knew I'd had enough.

I took my position in the raft. I stiffly gripped my paddle – my sword of defense now, not offense. My heart hammered, my responses were mechanical and slow. *Must get through this last one.* I don't remember much of this rapid beyond the roaring in my ears and confusion, and being tossed around the raft - but I stayed in it and we made it through to our lunch stop.

I was done for the day, I told Warren. I was hiking out. He offered to get me into a hold-on raft, but no, I had to quit. If I stopped now, I could quit while I was somewhat ahead (as in, alive). Warren was exceedingly disappointed in me. One guide flapped his wings at me, like a chicken.

I smiled. Call me coward, I care not. "That's me! I'm bailing!"

We all had lunch; then I ended up being the only one hiking out of the canyon. The three rafters that had paid for a half-day of rafting opted to stay for the full day; I was the only one who quit.

Fine with me. It was a long climb out, hot and strenuous, but I was very happy because I was hiking on solid ground and I was alive.

Give me the earth and mountains, I said in a prayer of thanks; *you people can have your raging rivers. I'll watch from the shore where I belong.* The men waiting at the top of the canyon to welcome and give the half-day-ers (only me) a ride back to Victoria Falls gave me not one, but two ice cold beers.

The mighty Zambezi river had brought me to my knees, but it let me survive.

I raised my beer in a toast to Nyami Nyami.

CANOEING THE ZAMBEZI RIVER

A three-day adventure

Two hundred miles down from Victoria Falls, the 450-foot-tall Kariba dam backs up the Zambezi river and forms Lake Kariba, a 170-mile reservoir. Dam construction began in 1955, when Zimbabwe was still Rhodesia, and it took four years. The dam controls 90% of the runoff from the Zambezi river.

With the building of the dam, 57,000 Zambezi Tonga people were also the recipients of the backup of the water which inundated their homes and land. They were relocated. In one writer's view, the Kariba dam was the worst dam-resettlement disaster in African history. But everybody needs power, right? Everybody wants progress, right? They were just some tribal African people, right?

But life changes and goes on. The lower part of this river was a food source for the people who lived here now, and an adventure source for a different industry. Below the dam is where we would begin our three-day canoe trip.

I was looking forward to a relaxing canoeing adventure down the gentle end of the river that tried to drown me white-water rafting below Victoria Falls.

<> <> <> <> <>

Day 1

Kariba Breezes was the name of our hotel and tour company that Janet booked our trip with. A truck was waiting at the hotel to transport the four of us to our put-in on the river below the Kariba dam.

Janet and Anthony, and their cousin Vicki, and I came here to continue our Zambezi adventure on canoes, after our wild rafting adventure.

We left our valuables at the hotel office, and left our car in the hotel parking lot. We'd pick it up at the end of our trip when we were driven back here.

Dave would be our tour guide on the river. This wasn't a part of the world you just rented a canoe and paddled away on your own. If you weren't familiar with the outdoors here, you might not come back.

We crowded into the back of a bakkie while a man drove Dave and us 20 minutes down the road to our drop-off site. Nobody told us we'd have a three-kilometer hike down to the river (we hadn't asked), but I loved it, even though it was godawful hot and humid. Porters carried most of our gear down the hills; we just carried our day packs with water and snacks.

Sweat poured off me as I followed nimble Dave down the trail, through a surprisingly green non-pine forest populated by, as far as we could see, baboons. Baboons will sometimes harass people, but fortunately these large primates ignored us.

Dave was well versed on the types of vegetation; he pointed out different trees and bushes and explained their uses. He was short and wiry, very muscular, delightfully affable. He oozed confidence, which is a quality you sure like to see in an adventure guide in an unfamiliar, wild part of the world.

Tsetse fly traps hung in trees in the area. These sub-Saharan blood suckers have long inspired terror, and are the biological vectors of trypanosomes which cause human sleeping sickness and animal trypanosomiasis. Untreated, the disease is fatal. It's still a thing nowadays, and the tsetse fly is actually ranked in some lists as one of the top five most deadly animals in

Africa.

"Tsetse" means "fly" in the Bantu language Tswana. It's rather scary-looking up close, with a long and wicked-looking proboscis.

Control techniques have improved over the decades, but they haven't eradicated the fly.

We arrived at our three waiting canoes lightly bobbing on the banks of the Zambezi river. Before we climbed aboard, Dave gave us The Talk.

First was a little history of the Zambezi, and what kind of animals we could expect to see. Only then did we find out we wouldn't likely see any big game because we'd be floating through a hunting reserve; therefore the animals would be very shy and cautious, even though it was currently off-season for hunting. We'd only likely see hippos, crocodiles, waterbuck, and impala.

And that brought us to The Safety Talk: what to do if a hippo attacks (wait - what?), what to do if a crocodile attacks (wait - what!?), neither of which sounded very appealing for us humans.

"If a hippo attacks your boat and flips it over – it's unlikely but possible, unless you're close to shore, stay with the boat. Try to climb on top of it." Ours were fiberglass canoes and weren't supposed to sink. "If the boat happens to get bitten in half, and you can't get on top, and you're close to shore, swim like hell." (Wait - WHAT!?) In other words, if you're not close to shore, well, basically, Kiss Your Ass Goodbye. If a hippo didn't get you, a crocodile would.

The other canoes - that is, the remaining ones of us hopefully still in our upright, whole canoes - would try to rescue you. "These are wild animals," Dave said. "Respect them, and they will respect you."

My eyes were wide as dinner plates. The four of us were very, very quiet.

Sufficiently alarmed, we loaded into our three canoes. I climbed in back of one (as the steerer) and Vicki crawled in front.

I was amazed how low the canoe sat to the water surface – like four inches; we were actually sitting below the water level – as compared to the rafts where you sat high above the river. I was a little uneasy at first, especially when the canoe wobbled, but after a few hours I had become very comfortable with it, and after another day, very proficient at stroking and steering. We wouldn't encounter any rapids on this part of the river, thank goodness! I'd take pretty much anything over rapids.

Shoving off from the bank, the gentle current tugged at us and started our float down the mighty-but-now-calmed Zambezi, past canyon walls rising among hills. We saw and passed our first crocodiles, sitting on the banks, seemingly docile, seemingly unmoving, but their eyes followed us. They gave me the creeps. Crocodiles can move fast enough on land, 11 miles an hour, and in water they can swim up to 18 miles an hour.

We approached a few clusters of hippos near the river banks. Sure, hippos are cute and funny, but they look a *whole* lot different when you are feeling very vulnerable, sitting four inches above the water in a piece of fiberglass in the middle of a big river full of crocodiles (and biting hippos). Hippos are considered among the most dangerous animals in the world with their aggressive and territorial and unpredictable nature. (Crocodiles also top of any lists of the deadliest animals in Africa behind the #1 Mosquito.)

When we floated closer to the hippos (and not even closely, because you absolutely do not want to get close to hippos in water), they turned to watch us with their beady little eyes. Sometimes they disappeared under water (were they swimming towards us??). When they got a bit agitated they started to snort. They sound a bit like horses when they do that. The name Hippopotamus amphibius comes from the Greek term for river horse.

Hippos have 'home bases,' though, and Dave knew where they were so we could avoid them. That made us feel a little better. "Unless," he added, "there's a lone bull, or one or two who've been kicked out of the herd." In which case they'll roam wherever they want. Oh. lovely. That made us feel a bit less better.

Already this was not just a lazy float down a pretty, quiet river. There were plenty of dangers, some obvious and some lurking whereabouts unknown beneath the surface of the water, that served to keep us on constant alert.

Despite that, though, if I could divert my attention from the potential sharp teeth below the surface, it was a lovely float down, sometimes paddling, sometimes drifting lazily with our three canoes hooked together (though never with any of our appendages dragging in the water, because - crocodiles), sometimes chatting, sometimes in companionable silence, listening to the rhythms of the African river and forest system.

We pulled out at a nice shady spot on the Zimbabwe side for a lunch: chicken/cheese sandwiches and bread. These plain sandwiches taste so very good when you're out in the wild. After we ate, some of us napped or read or walked around. It was sticky-humid and the flies were awful.

The wind suddenly kicked up; it clouded over rapidly, and we jumped up to pack the canoes, because rain was on the way. It hit just as we started down the river again. But we were wrapped in our raincoats, and it was a pleasant warm African rain.

After it cleared up 20 minutes later, it was so steamy hot. I used my cup to scoop water on myself. Why bother with the rain coat?

We saw several Zambian fisherman, who always waved and said hello, usually paddling upstream sitting or standing in their low, long dugout canoes.

We saw lots of fish ripples by our canoes that made me and Vicki flinch: "What was that! Dave! What is that!?"

Two Zambians thought Vicki and I were strong women for paddling our own canoe. They pointed at us and flexed their bicep muscles. Yes, we grinned and nodded, flexing our muscles and holding our paddles over our heads. (Apparently, Janet paddling with Anthony in their canoe didn't count as a strong woman, because obviously, he was the strong paddler.)

Around 5 PM we approached our designated island campsite, a short distance from a herd of hippos on the mainland. We could hear them a long way off – they sounded like noisy dirt bikes revving up. As we got close to our island - and our hippos – very near our pull-out site, they became obviously agitated: snorting, rearing in the water, some disappearing under, some popping up and huffing, beady eyes and big snouts just level with the water surface, always facing us. It was a bit nerve-racking, trying to follow Dave closely and maneuver to the shore while still staying as far away from the herd as possible.

Vicki and I got a bit tangled in tall weeds near the shore, and the hippos got even more agitated. The water separating us was a pretty narrow channel, looking even smaller as we got closer. Dave said, a little urgently, "This way girls," and he actually shoved his canoe into the bank, leaped out, and grabbed for our canoe, pulling it up to the bank, where we scrambled quickly out, all manner of calm demeanor out the window, almost relieved enough to kiss the ground. The hippos immediately quieted down as we left the water and moved onto higher ground away from them.

We four set up camp, unloading the canoes and setting up our tents, while Dave started cooking. We watched the hippos across the narrow strip of water, which, now that it was toward evening, were really waking up: yawning, two of them mating (or attempting to), sparring by seeing who had the wider mouth. One hippo splashed upstream through the shallow water and took a dump – a big sputtering and spraying of brown poop with his tail swishing around like a propeller.

A big male waterbuck strolled the river's shore, carefully approaching the water for a drink. He had a big white stripe, looking like a target, on his bum.

We dined on Dave's delicious beef stroganoff on rice, (lentils for Vicki the vegetarian), gem squash, carrots, wine, peanuts, chocolate. I felt like one of those white African explorers traveling an unmapped river but with the luxuries of civilization prepared for me.

In the background, the hippos yawned and hee-hawed and laughed like donkeys, and behind us a stunning sunset burnished the sky crimson. It was a hot night, but at least the mosquitoes weren't too bad.

At dark we took the flashlight and looked for crocodile eyes along the river bank. Dave warned us not to get close. We saw a few eyes and it was creepy! The crocodiles just sat there waiting, staring into the flashlight, unblinking, their eyes glowing red. I shivered.

Stars emerged, hanging like billions of beacons in the African sky. Dave told crocodile stories around the campfire. Six months ago he'd seen a guy eaten by a crocodile, a Zambian fisherman trying to get away from where they were fishing illegally. Their canoe turned over, and Dave said they could see the crocodile approaching, but there was nothing they could do. There was a short scream before the man was pulled under. They never found his body.

Crocodiles clamp down on their prey with their massive jaws filled with sharp teeth. National Geographic says their jaws can exert 3,700 pounds per square inch. They use a 'death roll' to kill their prey, grabbing it and pulling it down into the water, rolling and snapping their neck or drowning them. Supposedly a crocodile can't open its jaws easily against pressure; they can be held shut with a rubber band. Sounds a bit fishy, and not a fact I'd like to challenge.

The hippos had left the water around sunset, up the opposite bank on the mainland, for their night feeding. Hippos are primarily herbivores, preferring grasses, but they have been known to dine on carcasses. Also, they are fast. They can run 19 miles an hour on land despite their bulk. In the water, while they aren't known for being good swimmers, they move like ballerinas.

We could hear them all foraging around on the mainland and snorting over their dinners when we all went to bed at 9:30.

<> <> <> <> <>

Day 2

Vicki and I kept waking up in our tent during the night hearing strange noises... "What was that!?" "I don't know!" It was one thing to be scared by teeth lurking seen or unseen in the water in the daylight, but it was a different kind of scared in the African dark. The teeth were still out there but we didn't know what kind! I'd visited some game reserves, but we were always behind tall, sturdy fences listening to the African nights. Here only a thin canvas separated us from who knew what wild animals.

Noises were amplified in the dark. We heard hyaenas howl. We heard a hippo in the water. We heard what must've been a waterbuck in and near the water because of the dainty steps he took. We heard other thrashing in the water which must've been a crocodile. Did he maybe pull down and eat a waterbuck?

The hippo alarm woke us all up around 4:30 AM as they returned from their night of dining and carousing to the water, heehawing and making a big ruckus. We crawled out of our tents at 6 AM to a beautiful African sunrise.

I poked around our little island hunting rocks, while Dave made tea and coffee, and we all took turns with Douglas the Shovel off in the bushes.

We had our coffee, struck camp, packed the canoes, and headed downstream by 7 AM. We would stop later for breakfast, and get some paddling in while it was still pleasantly not-hot.

The river was much shallower and we had to follow Dave's wake exactly at some points so we wouldn't run aground on sand banks. The paddling and steering came naturally to me now. Vicki and I just naturally hit a rhythm with our stroking on opposite sides of the canoe.

It was a lovely morning, already warming quickly, though

a gentle breeze caressed the water. We passed several little crocodiles, miniature evil little buggers, sunning on the banks and watching us with their slitted eyes. Even baby crocodiles ooze menace.

We saw a big one, wickedly watching us. Our canoes all floated pretty close to him, and he didn't blink an eye nor move a muscle. Janet and Anthony's canoe got just a wee bit too close and *BAM* – he splashed into the water so fast and disappeared, if you'd have blinked, you'd have missed him.

Our hearts all lurched while Janet and Anthony paddled away from there very fast, and Dave scrambled to unpack his pistol! Vicki and I paddled quickly to the safe nearness of Dave's boat, putting him and Janet and Anthony between us and the submerged, invisible crocodile. I found my hands were shaking afterwards. "Guys, let's not get so close next time," Dave said. No need to worry about that!

We pulled out of the river on the Zambian side at 8:45 at a patch of shade for breakfast. Dave pulled out the cooking gear and the cooler and started on bacon and eggs, sausage and beans, while the rest of us wimps huddled under the trees out of the already-growing heat.

After breakfast, as we paddled on down the river, it starting getting seriously hot. Anthony and Janet had developed the runs, and we had to pull over for Anthony twice more, once on the Zambezi side, once on the Zimbabwe side, for a quick visit with Douglas. Janet's stomach was gurgling, and I tried to ignore the fact that mine was feeling a bit strange.

Noon crept past as we drifted downstream. It was now for sure damn hot. The sun was penetrating and severe and unforgiving. We all scooped water on ourselves continuously. The hours sluggishly rolled by on the Zambezi river.

We pulled off for a lunch stop under some big trees in Zambezi. Only Dave and I ate cheese sandwiches, and I had to rather stuff mine down. It was just too hot to want to eat. The flies were maddening.

Now it was stiflingly hot, even in the shade, at least 100

degrees or more, with at least 100% humidity. Janet, Anthony, and now Vicki were handing off Douglas like a relay and running to the bushes. I, instead of diarrhea (thank goodness) started my period in empathy with Janet and Vicki, though it was nowhere near its due time. Thank goodness Janet brought extra tampons on the trip!

I laid back and tried to snooze, but just trying to breathe the sultry air felt suffocating, even under shade. I covered my face with netting against the horrible flies, but they crept over the rest of me. I just gave in to them and let them crawl all over me because it was too unbelievably hot to care anymore or do anything about it. Anthony ran to the loo about four times.

We started off in the canoes again around 3 PM. I dunked everything I wore into the Zambezi. I covered up completely from the sun and kept pouring water on myself. That hot yellow disc was harsh and fierce, unrelenting. Even Dave said it was dreadfully hot.

We all wanted badly to swim – no chance at the lunch site - and Dave told us to pull up to a sandbank island we were passing. Anthony was miserable with diarrhea. We were all wilting, the sun beating us to shreds.

"There's a wallow pool here," said Dave. As we pulled the canoes onto the island, we jumped in the little pool (it was not too deep, and we were always watching out for crocodiles), and we bathed and wallowed and gloried for over a half hour. We shampooed and soaped and laid there (with somebody always on watch). I'd never had such a great bath before. I felt sparklingly clean after a wash in the dirty Zambezi.

Refreshed for a while, we paddled onward.

We came to a slightly hairy spot in the river that got our collective adrenaline pumping. Hippos on the right in the water, watching us. Hippos on the left in the water, getting a little agitated. Crocodiles on the left now, too; we got a little nervous. And more hippos to the right.

We followed Dave's moves exactly. Paddle quickly, and straight, don't angle towards them! Vicki and I hung right by

Dave's canoe, almost close enough to bump him, and we paddled strongly to pass the hippos. We did *not* want to take a dip around here. Thankfully we emerged from the danger zone, and stayed close to the Zimbawe banks, because poor Anthony had to stop again and again to run behind a bush with Douglas.

We passed many Zambians fishing and paddling upstream. They all waved at us and went about their fishing business. On the Zambian side, conical mud huts with pointed thatched roofs occasionally dotted the forest in small groups.

We floated out of the hills and mountains into flat land and swamps. Where the Zambezi spread out half a mile wide, we picked a path through murky water, reeds, and canals (*surely* full of lurking crocodiles), and stopped on a lovely sandy bank of an island to camp for the night.

A lone waterbuck stood watching us on a hill – a beautiful picture – but I only got one shot before Anthony had to run towards him with his own call of nature.

We set up camp again, and enjoyed refreshing ice-cold beer from the cooler. I was pooped, from the baking heat and the occasional tension/entertainment provided by the African wildlife. Dave cooked. He never ran out of energy, was constantly cheerful. It wasn't put-on; you could tell he was a content fellow, and he loved what he was doing.

Anthony got some rehydrating solution that Dave had brought along in the first aid kit, and kept running off with Douglas, hoping the electrolytes would help soon.

As the evening cooled down we were blessed with a much-welcomed cooling breeze, and fireworks of distant lightning at sunset.

Dinner was delicious spaghetti bolognese. There's something about eating food that someone else prepares for you in the wilderness, though I think Dave's cooking would have tasted great anywhere.

Janet and Anthony went to bed; Vicki and I sat up with Dave around the campfire and talked about things. He'd been a guide for six years now (he's 32), and he still loved his job.

You could tell, by the way he did everything, how he knew and pointed out his animals and birds, the way he talked about the animals with a respect born from experience.

It was Another Shit (Hot) Day in Africa, as Anthony always likes to say, because it always is hot in Africa in the summer.

Vicki and I looked again for crocodile eyes in the dark while we brushed our teeth. One just sat across the water on the banks and watched us. So spooky!

<> <> <> <> <>

Day 3

Funny thing – first thing upon awakening this morning, I had a rather strange twinge of fear and an I-don't-want-to-face-the-hippos-and-crocs-today feeling. But what are you going to do? We had to paddle down the Zambezi. Surely it was just my imagination getting the better of me.

I heard Anthony get up and run to the loo two of his 10 times during the night. I got up first around 6 AM and just sat and soaked up and inhaled another wild African early morning. It *smelled* like Africa: dirt, river, wildness, humidity, heat. Already it was unbelievably hot.

After the rest crawled out of their tents, Dave had said we'd have breakfast here and we'd shove off at 9, but he just made coffee and decided after all that we'd go downstream to seek some shade for breakfast.

We floated downriver. It was incomprehensibly hot already. Unbelievable, oppressing heat and humidity. Stultifying, stupefying, staggering heat. How many words can I find to describe the African heat? Because it was all of that. At times it was such an effort to lift the paddle. Sometimes we just floated, collapsed, wilted, shriveled up, baked in our canoes. Anyone wants to torture me, all they have to do is take me to Kariba and down the Zambezi river in summer for a week and I'd confess, or make up anything they wanted to hear.

We paddled down the wide river, giving plenty of space to hippos and a few crocodiles – lots of babies on the banks – here and there.

We were in the middle of a very wide part of the Zambezi when we approached many hippos – at least two (that we could see) on the right, and about 50 (!) on the left. There was no way to go completely around the whole two groups. We would have to split them. I had a bad feeling about this, and my heart started unbidden lurching in my chest.

The two hippos on the right watched us, then dove under. Vicki and I gulped, and instinctively started to paddle strongly. We three canoes crowded closely together and picked up the paddle tempo even more. This was no time to dawdle, in the middle of the mile-wide river.

The massive hippo pod on the left was suddenly and quickly disturbed – snorting, popping up and down in the water. Our canoes were crammed close together, bumping occasionally, Dave slightly in the lead. Dead silent but for our five paddles kissing the water and the huffing hippos. Nothing needed to be said. We all knew this was a bad situation and we needed to get the hell out of there.

The two hippos on the right were still under water – where the hell were they?! The pack on the left, that we were now too close to, were agitated, though we didn't dare veer any closer to the two underwater ones.

The biggest hippo in front of the big herd swam toward us with purpose and dove underwater. *Oh, shit.*

It wasn't what Dave said, it was the way he said it: "Guys, paddle." He murmured it quietly, save-your-life seriously.

If the hippo came up under our canoes, or one was bitten in two - and Dave had just finished telling us about that happening – we were in serious shit. We were in the middle of the Zambezi River, nearly a half mile from either shore. If you swim, it's Kiss Your Ass Goodbye. For me it was equal the terror of white-water rafting, only terror on a completely different plane.

"Ohhh" said Vicki.

"Just paddle," I hissed, because I was terrified to death, my heart ping-ponging out of my chest, my breath choked, and we threw our paddles into the Zambezi and prayed with every stroke and pulled for our lives. In the same river, I paddled harder than I did white -water rafting, and I prayed harder. We dug and strained held our breaths and looked only forward, not daring to glance at the water, not wanting to see a hippo coming up underneath one of us, dreading that *bump* of a canoe, and *ohmigod we were going to die.*

Nothing happened. We glided away swiftly, and finally ventured a look back. The hippos were still watching and snorting; the big one on the left was still under water, somewhere. The two on the right were still under water, somewhere. We didn't let up, all of us concentrating on power and speed and distance.

We didn't ease up until we got to a shallower sand bar half a mile down the river. I broke the silence. "Jaysus!" It all hit me at once and my hands shook so violently I dropped my paddle in the boat. I felt like crying.

"Shit!" said Vicki.

"What scared us," Janet croaked, "was the tone of your voice!"

"Yea, well," Dave said, smiling, ever cheerful, "I was a little worried when that big one started charging. I about shat myself."

We all let off terrific laughs, a great release of tension, not even wanting to think about the What Ifs. We were still alive to happily continue experiencing another Shit (Hot) Day in Africa.

<> <> <> <> <>

We paddled over a lot of shallows that looked so safe and inviting. It was so, so hot. The pools would have felt so refreshing, but we knew crocodiles were watching and waiting for human morsels.

We could see Chirundu, our end-point, not far away. We pulled over on the side of Zimbabwe, and Dave made us another fried breakfast.

Anthony and Vicki took turns running to the loo; Janet's stomach still gurgled. I was fine. Lucky, lucky me – unless it just hadn't hit yet. Maybe my paranoia for drinking purified water, always dropping iodine tablets in my water bottle, was paying off.

We tossed our leftover food scraps in the water, and the little fish went nuts over them. I tried to get the fish to come take bites from off my fingers. They would think about it, come within two inches, then chicken out and dart away. The shore dropped off rapidly so we had to watch for crocodiles.

Far offshore were a pile of hippos. Speed boats would zoom by, probably bothering the hippos enough to where one day they'd take it out on some innocent canoers, like us. The hippos heehawed and snorted and splashed in their distant pile.

We packed up one last time, and in the blazing heat, paddled downstream to Chirundu and our pull-out site. The river was narrower here, and for a while we hugged the Zambian side. We had to walk the canoes through some very shallow spots, and Dave and I did quick lay-downs in the water to cool down.

Anthony had to stop again for the loo, followed by Vicki. It was bloody hot, mind-numbing heat that made you just not give a fart about anything. It sapped our will. We were coming to the end of this amazing canoe adventure on the Zambezi river... but we just couldn't care much. It was like giving in to the terrible flies, you surrendered to the heat and let it overwhelm and numb you because there was nothing else to do about it.

I kept scooping the now-dirty-brown water on me constantly. We pulled up to the boat ramp about noon, and alas, our canoe trip was over. I could've gone on another four days, although maybe at a cooler time of year, and now that the ice in our coolers was melted, and without cold drinks during the day, my thirst would never have been quenched and I would have suffered. Iced drinks on this trip were so decadent and necessary!

We waited for our transport back to Kariba; it arrived at 12:30 with more canoes and a party of 10. We looked like hell, and we couldn't help but notice and laugh at how clean the new folks were. We jumped right in to help Dave and the other guides unload and load canoes, while the new tourists stood around unsure of what was ahead.

They stared at us, wet, grotty, dirty, wearing all sorts of combinations of khoi khois, shirts, hats, bandanas, we, the veteran explorers of a wild adventure on the Zambezi river.

CHAPTER 4:
SCOTLAND, 1993

Time slows down here

Why Scotland? Why the western and northern islands of the island nation of Scotland?

I'm really a mountain person. Oceans, beaches don't particularly interest me that much. Yes indeed, the isle of Scotland is surrounded by islands and full of ocean beaches. But something about those green island(s) in the Atlantic Ocean intrigued me.

And, because two years earlier I had met Scottish Kirsty at a youth hostel in Hong Kong. Along with Wanda from Canada, we hung out together for a week there.

I had a standing invitation from Kirsty to come visit her family in Scotland, and her in England any time.

I'd long had my eye on Ireland, for its rich horse racing history, and it would make total sense to combine Scotland, Northern Ireland, Ireland, and England in a three-month-long trip.

And so, I went to Scotland.

THE SCOTTISH ISLES - TOWARD

September 29

Kirsty was in London; I'd see her later in my travels when we'd go to Royal Ascot together to watch the horse races. Right now, it was Scotland first, and visiting Kirsty's home and family in Toward (rhymes with Howard), a little village 30 miles west of Glasgow, reachable by car and ferry.

Kirsty's mom was going to pick me up at the Glasgow airport, but after breezing through customs, I didn't see anybody looking for an obvious backpack traveler.

Just as I was about to look into a bus to the Wilsons' place, I heard my name paged in the airport.

This was Mrs. Bobbie Wilson paging me, and she gathered me up and whisked me straight off to her car. Outside, Scotland was gray and raining, just like Seattle. Bobbie finally stopped apologizing for the weather ("It was nice up until this morning!") when she realized I didn't care, and in fact enjoyed dismal, rainy weather. "It's just like home," I assured her. "I love it!"

Old stone fences lined the roads that everyone drove on the wrong side of. I kept wanting to reach over and take the wheel and jerk us over to the right side. I was so excited to be in Scotland!

We caught the short car ferry across the Firth of Clyde to Kirn and Dunoon; and after stopping at Wilson's Garage and

Repair Shop to show me off to some cousins, and at a fruit and veggie store, we drove the few miles down small local roads along the water to Toward, and Kirsty's cute little family box house.

Bobbie plied me with a refreshing snack of tea and crackers, then I was invited to go with Uncle Neil and Stuart (Mr. Wilson's General Manager and CEO – they seemed to have a very successful garage) to move the Wilson's boat to safer mooring over the winter. Ride a boat on the frigid water in winter? Count me in!

My travel plans to head to and up the Outer Hebrides, then to the Orkneys and Shetlands, were always met with, well, askance, especially when I said, "I may do the northern islands in December." It was general consensus that I was brave (or totally ignorant), and that if I were to do any islands, I should do the northern ones first, before the real winter weather arrived.

I had of course planned to find my way to the islands myself, but oh no, Bobbie had already taken care of everything. Though she and her husband Jack would leave tomorrow for a week's vacation in Malta, they would find me a ride to Oban where, at their Esso plant, I'd find their secretary Rosemary, and she'd help me arrange ferry transport to and through the Outer Hebrides.

Meanwhile throughout the day, Bobbie was talking about Kirsty's brother Muddy, and I kept thinking, how could anybody name their kid Muddy! Maybe it had to do with the always-damp Scotland.
Finally I had to ask her to spell it. M-u-r-r-a-y. I heard Muddy! I should've figured that out, because I was "Meddi" to everybody here I was introduced to.

Bobbie fed me tomato soup, then I sat to read and wait for Stuart and Uncle Neil. I dozed off for half an hour – I was at about 24 hours of sleeplessness – when they arrived at the house at 4 PM. We drove down the road a ways to the water, changed into serious ain't-messing-around waterproof Atlantic fishing gear, and rowed out to their Americruiser.

It took us half an hour to motor the boat to the new mooring right at the Kirn ferry landing, as only one engine was working. I was getting a bit groggy, but here I was, riding a boat, up the Firth of Clyde, in Scotland! It wasn't too cold, only around 45 degrees, but boy that water was icy. Even covered from head to toe, with only my eyes and nose and mouth poking out of the raincoat hood, the ocean spray made me shiver. I can swim, but I'd have died of instant cold shock if I'd fallen in.

Jack picked us up, and drove like a maniac to get us home, 70 miles an hour on the little winding roads. Blind curves were really scary because I always wanted to yell, "You're on the wrong side of the road!"

Back home was Helen, a friend who would watch the house while the Wilsons were away, and three dogs, Stumpy, Cody, and big fat black Inky who snores, even while he's awake. We ate a big dinner of roast and potatoes, followed by strawberries doused in pure cream, sugar and liqueur, and I went to bed – going on 36 awake hours now – piled under blankets, and crashed.

<> <> <> <> <>

September 30

I woke up in…. Scotland! I left my drapes open last night, and from the upstairs room, the windows overlooked the front yard, cows in a green pasture across the road, the Firth of Clyde, and the Scottish mainland beyond.

Bobbie woke me at 8:30 to say goodbye; Helen would pick me up in the afternoon and take me to Inveraray, where they found a bus that would take me to Oban, where I was to find Rosemary at their offices there. She gave me an extra map, to go with the extra hostel information she'd picked up for me, and a wool sweater and a small sleeping bag of Kirsty's she insisted I take with me. I could leave it with Kirsty in London.

After they left, I crawled back into bed and slept luxuriously until 10 AM. I got up and walked into the kitchen welcomed by beating doggie tails on the floor, and I cooked a breakfast of bacon (their bacon here is so thick and fatless it's like heavenly ham) and egg and toast and instant coffee with pure cream. The doggies got their share too.

Helen arrived at 1:30 and drove me the hour to Inveraray, giving me the guided tour along the way. Sandbank, just north of Dunoon, was where, up until a year ago, the Americans kept a nuclear sub base. Yesterday Uncle Neil pointed out the black outlines on the rocks and shores at high tide made by the oil expelled from warships in the 1940s.

It was partly cloudy, with rain expected, of course, and the leaves on the trees are beginning to change to golden colors. We drove along many lochs, salt or freshwater: alongside Lock Eck, and around the top of Loch Fyne into Inveraray, where Helen insisted on buying me ice cream and waiting with me for the bus to Oban. "If it doesn't arrive, I'll drive you on to Oban."

A brisk, shivery wind whipped up Loch Fyne, presumably to give me a foretaste of the Outer Hebrides I'm headed for.

The bus showed up right on time. I gave Helen a hug and jumped aboard, and the friendly bus driver drove us the hour to Oban. I reflected on the utter ease and comfort I'd experienced so far. Everyone had been extremely friendly and gone out of their way to help me; the luxurious, comfortable bus was clean, airy, no rattling windows or blaring video, there were only half a dozen people aboard, and, the bus driver used his brakes, all unlike some places where I've traveled. I almost felt guilty about it, but... I was enjoying the lack of travel stress immensely. I deserved it after the time I've put in riding some third-world-country buses.

After following Loch Awe, then Lock Etive, we descended from a small hill into Oban on the Firth of Lorn, "Gateway to the Hebrides."

I found and checked into Jeremy Inglis' hostel, where I walked in the door at the same time with two Aussie girls. The talkative and friendly Jeremy gave us all a dorm room together.

I dumped my now-heavier pack and hiked back into town

and wandered around for a while. I like to get a feel for places by walking the streets without a map, though maps weren't necessary in these small towns.

Back at the hostel, Tabitha and Katherine and I decided to go back out for tea. Once we got to the Oban Inn we opted instead for pints of beer, and the mostly men in the pub ogled us as we sipped and talked. When we walked out, they hollered, "Whatsa matter girls, we men too much for ya?"

After that, Catherine wanted to go to the Poop Deck pub, because just the name was enough to draw us there. We escaped upstairs when some strange over-imbibed under-sexed young men gave us a hard eye. We sipped our brews in peace and talked about life in America and Australia and traveling. We were back in the hostel and in bed by 9 PM.

THE SCOTTISH ISLES – THE OUTER HEBRIDES

October 1
South Uist

Outer Hebrides, here I come! My ferry to Lochboisdale on South Uist left at 3 PM. The aptly named *Lord of the Isles* sailed up the Sound of Mull, with the mainland, Morvern, to our right, and the island of Mull to the left. Everything was changing colors like a live painting: the sky a dozen shades of blue, the water a dozen shades of gray, and, at places, clear sky with sun teasing through. Tall hills rose straight up out of the water, mostly bright green, flecked with many shades of brown, under dark skies streaked blue, even purple, with the hills changing to gray at the tops, blending into the hanging clouds. Further land masses were a dark blue. The water itself transformed as we churned forward, from gray to blue, to green or colorless under the sun, and, when we entered the sea of Hebrides, a deep, moody, dark blue-gray.

Leaving Mull and the mainland behind, we passed the islands of Coll and Tiree to the left, and Muck, Eigg, Rum and Canna to the right. Don't you think it would be fun to say, "I live on Muck!"

Ahead of us was nothing but sea. I spent a lot of time outside – it wasn't too terribly cold – having to run either around the back of the ship or through it from side to side and craning my neck out over the rails because all observation areas were in back of the boat. I wanted to see where we were going; I wanted to see it all!

Once in the sea of Hebrides, I grabbed a window chair and dozed for half an hour, and when I woke, the Hebrides were just appearing ahead through the rainy skies. The sea wasn't too rough but the boat gently rocked back and forth, and would occasionally shudder and bump, as if we'd run over a rock in the road or a whale underneath the water. I have no fear (yet) on boats, though if we started sinking, I'd probably pass out from terror.

It was dark by the time we docked at at Lochboisdale on South Uist. It didn't seem like many people disembarked; whoever did was gone quickly. I walked alone in the dark, towards buildings, not sure exactly where I'd go or what I'd do (the man at the ferry ticket office said the bus northward left in the morning), but strangely unconcerned. After all, this wasn't India! And it wasn't raining, nor was it cold.

Up ahead was a lighted building. It was the tourist office and it was open! I was their only customer. They called on the phone for me, then pointed the way to a nearby B & B owned by Mrs. MacLellan.

I walked up the road to Mrs. M's house, nothing fancy, just a simple house on the island. She showed me to a room with two single beds, pointed out the bathroom and a teapot by my bed with a good supply of tea and coffee bags, and said she'd have breakfast ready at 8:30 AM.

After a cup of tea, and chewing on dry bread, cheese, and biscuits (thank goodness I had that – it was all I'd eaten since the chicken leg I ate at the ferry terminal in Oban), I wrote in my journal, and pulled out my maps and brochures for the Hebrides and Shetlands and Orkneys. It was quite a chore and responsibility, trying to figure out where to go and how to get there, what the bus or ferry schedules were, how and where to obtain food along the way.

But it didn't matter, because I was on the Outer Hebrides of Scotland!

<> <> <> <> <>

October 2
South Uist

Once I finally fell asleep, I was out like a light in that nice warm bed. When my alarm went off I didn't want to get up, especially when I heard the wind howling outside. I had to smile – welcome to the Hebrides!

I wasn't sure if Mrs. M was going to get me, or if I was to wander about the house in search of the kitchen, or wait until I was sure she was awake. What was the protocol here? It was my first time in a B & B, and I wasn't sure how to act. B & Bs are normally way above my traveler's budget (or mindset). I was living the high life here and I didn't want to mess it up.

At 8:40 I crept out my door and into the living room, timidly said, "Hello?"

"Morning! Yes! Come sit!" Mrs. M pointed to my place at the table and said help myself to cereal; then she brought toast, a plate of ham/bacon, sausage, egg, and tomatoes, and coffee.

She left me alone to eat, and after I devoured all my food and coffee and finished staring out her windows onto the wet and windy bay, it was time to walk back to the ferry landing for the bus.

I said goodbye and left her house, stepping out into the wind and rain, wearing my raincoat. By the time I reached the tourist office, I was plenty wet. There I donned my rain pants (which would have been more effective *before* I got my pants wet) and pulled out my poncho to cover my packs. Great idea, stuffing that poncho in my backpack at home, at the last minute.

It was a short walk to the ferry, where the nice ferry men let me wait inside the waiting room; and when the bus bound for Howmore pulled up at 10 AM, I hopped on.

"Nice day, eh?" the nice bus driver said. He wasn't being sarcastic; it was an affable greeting. I sat across from a friendly lady who'd lived on the island for 30 years.

The A865 that runs all the way up to North Uist is a paved, single-lane road with little 'passing areas' where cars meet each other. I saw one tree, that's *one* tree, the whole 12-mile trip, and that was a scraggly, wind-beaten, twisted-limbed leafless trunk that had fought for and earned every day of its life on that island.

When the driver dropped me off at Howmore and pointed me up the road toward the hostel, it had stopped raining, though the wind still blew a gale.

From my rough sketch of a map on a brochure Jeremy had given me, I found the thatched-roof hostel after a half-mile hike, and a German boy inside.

I parked my pack and we chatted a while, then I went back outside on a walk northward up the beach. It would have been much more pleasant to sit inside; but the outdoors, the elements, the sea, pulled me outside. The wind howled and blew, and although there were no rain clouds above me drops continued to fall, so I pulled out my poncho. But trying to get that thing on in the gale was one grand giggle. It's like the Law of Tarps: whenever you want to fold up a tarp, the wind blows and it's almost impossible. When you want to put on a rain poncho, the wind blows and it's almost impossible. Once I wrestled it on, it kept me dry enough and also served as a great windbreaker.

The Atlantic Ocean wasn't anything spectacular at that moment in time, although the power and immensity of oceans - they cover about 70% of the earth's surface - never cease to amaze me. And all those waves – what are they doing? Where do they come from? Where are they going? Why? What determines their size? They seem to have such a purpose. They are like an ongoing conversation.

The beach was littered with a ton of stinky kelp. A man rode past me on a motorcycle, then got off and walked purposefully to and through the kelp. What was he looking for?

I walked an hour up the beach leaning left into the wind, and an hour back, leaning right into the wind. I walked past the hostel, back up to the A865 and to the little store. Tomorrow is

Sunday, and, I was told, things don't happen much on Sundays here. The islands of North Uist, Harris, and Lewis are strictly Catholic, and strictly observe the Sabbath, and the store won't be open, and buses won't be running, although the ferry does leave from Lochboisdale in the morning.

I loaded up on a can of tuna, lentils, rice, and potatoes, and I bought their last onion. For lunch at the hostel, I made tuna with mustard from the common cupboard; the mustard was so dang hot it made my nose run and eyes water and throat constrict. I think I breathed fire. That English mustard was powerful!

By now the sun was out and I just couldn't sit inside, so I started off on a short walk southward down the beach, which turned into a long walk, still buffeted by the gales. After another hour, I passed more nasty, stinky beds of kelp almost two feet thick, a rather wimpy (modern?) standing stone, and many bunny rabbits. When I made a whistle like a hawk they ran, but I think they were just plain running. I haven't seen any hawks here anyway. The wind probably blows them back to the mainland if they try to visit South Uist.

I came back to the hostel and sort of 'washed up,' if that's what you call a quick rub down with soap and a towel from an icy cold faucet.

I met the other fellow staying here, a Scotsman from Edinburgh. "M' name's Pot," he said with a nod. With my now-commanding knowledge of the Scottish accent I knew he meant "Pat." I thought I could detect a difference in the Edinburgh vs. Glasgow accent.

Hoping the sunset would be gorgeous, I went back outside to try some photos, though it wasn't as brilliant as it looked like it was going to be. It did make a minor attempt to be flashy at the last minute, with pink and lavender pastel hues.

Back at the hostel I cooked a lentil dish with fried potatoes – the lentils were great because I was tired and hungry. And anyway, everything tastes so much better when you're traveling. These hostel kitchens were so convenient, and necessary, in these small villages with no restaurants.

The hostel has one room with two beds, one room with six beds (and plenty of room for cots), a kitchen area where we keep a slow coal fire in the stove burning (four gas cookers), a separate area to wash dishes, and a bathroom.

German Harri and Scottish Pat were also here cooking when the warden Betty MacDonald stopped in, a cheery older lady whose mother retired from being the hostel warden at the age of 80, after 37 years.

These hostels are such a great idea: 3.65 pounds a night to experience the Hebrides in a comfortable, sheltered, simple Scottish island dwelling.

I boiled a pot of water to do dishes; afterwards I bundled up and sat outside in the dark, sipping coffee, listening to Howmore, South Uist: a few rain drops, wind, (which had died down considerably), sheep, a lone car, voices, distant waves. The almost-full moon was trying to peek through fluffy clouds, and temperature-wise, it was a mild night, in the upper 50's. It was peaceful, and I was right where I was supposed to be at that moment.

Pat said he was going to walk up Beinn Mhòr ("Big Hill") tomorrow. It's the highest point on South Uist, at 2,431 feet. I asked him if I could come along, because just today I was looking up there from the beach, thinking, it's not that high, and what a great view it must have.

I found out that the wimpy standing stone I saw along the north beach was indeed a real one, marked on Pat's map. Also marked are "Danger Areas" lining the beaches that I walked – both directions – where the army fires missiles. Now they tell me.

We have the broken remnants of a missile behind our abode, about six feet long, and 25 inches around, tail span almost the length of my arms.

<> <> <> <> <>

October 3
South Uist

I woke up at 8:20 (Pat had wanted to leave on our hike at 8:30) but fortunately he spent half an hour looking for his rain pants, so I had time for coffee and a quick breakfast of bread and jam.

We struck out at nine. I went prepared for conquering a Scottish peak, wearing sweats and sweatshirt, and carrying every piece of rain gear I had, and wearing my Gore-tex hiking shoes, which I've lived in since I arrived in Scotland. My feet were bruised from walking on the beach and rocks yesterday, but I figured, if you keep whaling on bruises long enough, they won't hurt anymore.

I reckoned rightly from the beginning this would be no simple stroll when, starting out on the road, Pat's strides left me behind and I had to push just to keep up with his flat walking pace. I'm not a slow hiker, but I felt like we were on a mission march. But I couldn't very well tell him to slow down, since he agreed I could tag along! So I sucked it up and marched, breathing heavily.

Studying our map, we chose a place to leave the paved road and started walking up a rocky muddy track. It was of course windy, and so far mostly sunny, but on the upper reaches of Beinn Mhòr perched a gray cloud hat with its own special surprises. At some point we left the track which ran out among the carved gulches, through the swampy heather-covered ground, where people dug up peat. It's kind of like strip mining in a way; it damaged the landscape in its own way, and made it a bitch for us to cross.

We leaped boldly from heather patch to heather patch, trying to avoid sinking into bogs or getting our boots too wet. The wind continued a steady 20 to 25 miles an hour in our faces, and it wasn't easy going, jumping here and hopping there and me having to fast-march over the six-inch to foot-high heather bushes. I had seen a postcard of some hills covered in brilliant purple heather in the springtime. It must be stunning. Now, without the showy purple flowers, it was only tiring.

And Pat – well, the inclines didn't slow or shorten his stride one iota; in fact the spring in his steps increased, and much to my annoyance he would leap upwards, while I felt like I was clambering on all fours. My lungs were about to burst as though I were at 15,000 feet instead of 1,500 feet. But my pride still wouldn't allow me to ask him to slow down!

The cloud hat still perched above us obscuring the peak, and it was, in fact, lower now. What, I wondered, goes on in one of those little gray top hat clouds that sits on the top of a mountain? I was about to find out.

I was unreasonably tired (although I was definitely pushing myself, well beyond my normal pace), but heck, I was this far, and even though there would be no view, there was no sense in *not* going to the top. We slowly ascended and disappeared into the cloud, and our immense, great view slowly faded, until we were socked inside this hat cloud. The wind picked up, mist swirled all around us, and we continued up, seeing no more than 20 feet in front of us.

The wind must have been a steady 45 miles an hour, and when it whipped up the eastern slopes, over the top and down over us, it gusted up to 60 miles an hour. It actually knocked me off my feet once. Spectacular Scottish island wind!

We had passed a rock cairn just before we entered the cloud, and we reached another one at the top where we added a stone. No point in staying on top in the wind and moisture (we couldn't even hear each other yell), so we headed right back down, back out of the mist cloud and hurricane, across the heather and boggy swamps in the normal wind, eventually back to the road. The sky was slowly clouding over, so we timed it well, getting up and down when we did.

The local store happened to be open, and we stopped in for goodies, then got back to the hostel at 2:30. My head was throbbing with a headache, probably from fighting that wind and forcing myself on an off-hiking day up the little local 'hill' following a spry Scotsman with giant strides. I took off my hiking boots, treated myself to coffee and aspirins and candy, 'washed' off, and planted myself inside for the rest of the day.

Two Germans were smooching on the couch when Pat and I got back, and they said they wanted to go climb Beinn Mhòr. "Have fun!" I said. By now it looked a bit stormy, but they went anyway, and later it turned windier, cooler, and rainy. We kept an eye out as evening approached, to make sure they made it back.

Another new guy, Scottish Paul, came in and had some tea; over-abundant-energy Pat went for another walk back to the store, then Paul's wife Meg and two-year-old son Thomas joined us. They didn't want to camp in the rain tonight. They're from the Isle of Skye and on a nine-day holiday.

We all cooked together, talked, and shared food. The Germans returned at 7 PM rather weather-shorn, having crawled halfway up the mountain before turning around and staggering back down.

Paul traded me an onion for some garlic cloves, Pat shared his yummy candy bars, and I shared my tea bags.

The warden Betty MacDonald showed up to collect money. She's such a nice lady; first thing she mentioned again was the weather. Harri asked me yesterday when I said she had popped in, "Did she talk about the weather?"

Well, yes, she did. Harri said, "That's the favorite topic of conversation of all the Islanders." It does seem to be, since it is such an integral part of life on the island.

<> <> <> <> <>

October 4
Berneray

Pat decided to catch the bus with me and head to the little island of Berneray. Covering just over six square miles, it's probably been inhabited since the Stone Age, and is the birthplace of the giant Angus MacAskill, whom we shall run into later.

After stocking up on toffee and candy bars at the store, the bus picked us up at 10:30 and took us to the airport on Benbecula, a tiny island sandwiched between North and South Uist, linked by road. I saw my first Scottish horses on Benbecula, a fuzzy Shetland and a fuzzy black bigger pony.

From the airport we caught the little red post bus (a common means of travel for people on these islands) to Lochmaddy on North Uist. The two old women on the bus conversed in Gaelic. Out here on the islands, it sometimes feels like I'm traveling in a very foreign land.

The bus dropped us in Lochmaddy at 12:30; the bus to the ferry landing to Berneray wasn't until 8 PM, so Pat said he'd start walking and hitch it. "How far is it?" I asked, just in case we didn't get a ride.

"Oh, five miles or so." I had seen his map, and I thought it looked like a lot more than five miles. But I said, yea sure, why not. I can lug this ridiculously heavy pack a couple of hours, no problem.

Pat walked well ahead (easy with that huge stride of his) to give me the chance to hitch a ride first. How Scotsmanly gentlemanly of him. I didn't argue.

I let a few cars pass before I tried timidly sticking out my thumb. Hitchhiking was also a normal way for travelers to get around on these islands, but it was sure new for me!

I got used to cars going past and ignoring me (many were full of people), and finally after an hour of walking, about three miles, a lorry stopped. Yahoo! He was a jolly chap hauling coal and tar, and he only took me a couple of miles before he turned off, but it was a great lift, especially mentally.

On the next leg, maybe a whole two cars passed me, ignoring my thumb. I walked for what seemed to be more than two hours, had to be another six miles (see? It was much further than five miles), keeping up a good steady pace. My pack wasn't too much heavier, and at least the weather was fine – no rain and no wind.

But by now things were rubbing: the back of my heels, and under my right ham, which was very annoying and uncomfortable. And I was soaked from head to toe in sweat.

Well the road went on and on, and I knew I had to be getting close to the ferry point, and I heard a car coming and I thought, I know I'm almost there, but, please pick me up?

She did! Inside was Pat, and I gratefully threw in my packs and crawled in. She wasn't even going to Berneray; she just drove out of her way and gave us a short ride to the ferry.

She dropped us off, and while waiting in the ferry room, another Scottish woman arrived. We expected the little ferry at 3 PM, in 10 minutes – we could see it, parked at the island of Berneray, which was in swimming distance if anyone dared to brave the frigid water and currents – but it never came. Turns out they had just started the winter schedule today, so there was no 3 PM ferry. We'd have to wait longer.

I found a bathroom, where I peeled off my sweat-soaked socks and jeans, pulled out the bandaids and put them on the raw spots, and switched to tennis shoes and shorts and sweats. Travel Rule #3: Never, never, do a 10-mile (or more) hike with a 250-pound pack in jeans. You get raw skin at the most inconvenient places.

The 4:45 ferry took less than five minutes to cross the water to Berneray; this was the car ferry which docked further away than the passenger ferry, so we had yet *another* three-mile hike to the hostel. At least I hoped this one was just three miles.

Well, somehow on this quick ferry ride over, my pack had gained another 100 pounds. Funny how that works with backpack traveling, when you don't even add anything to your pack.

Pat and I stopped at a tiny store, where a jolly old Scottish man and his wife greeted us and talked to us. He and his wife had "been married 40 years come Christmas Eve," he said, as he reached out and tousled her hair. "Had to go to Skye to get her."

He was quite proud of his island, and said, "Make sure you visit the sand dunes on the other side. Grand weather, 'tis."

Everybody waved as we walked past them; the Scottish woman on the ferry said around 120 people live here now.

The last two miles were painful. I felt like such a wimp! Pat slowed down and stayed with me although I tried to get him to stride on ahead.

I was never so happy to see that hostel as it appeared ahead, two white, simple thatched-roof cottages right on the shore. Nobody but some backpacks were around, and while Pat bounded right back out to go hike around, I went straight for the wash room. The shower looked tempting, and it *said* it had hot water, but I remembered Harri from Howmore saying that it took ten minutes just to get wet, and it was cold water. So it was the cold washcloth-off trick again and it still wasn't really refreshing, but I tried.

This hostel has three dorm rooms, one attached to the common room/kitchen, and two in a separate building. I went to the common room where I met two English girls who had been here nine days. Nine days on this tiny island!

I made myself some tea, warmed up my leftover fried potatoes, and washed clothes in hot water in the sink.

One of the wardens, Jessie, came in (apparently she has a twin, Ann), a sweet old lady who collects the food scraps for her chickens. She collected my money and stamped my hostel book, then left, saying, "Bye, dodgy out." A fitting, common phrase used on the islands. The going was "dodgy," the weather was "dodgy." Certainly, my body is "dodgy."

Later I met the two other guys staying here, Lawrence from England and Doug from South Africa. Lawrence had also been here nine days or so, and Doug had been here two weeks, then went to Howmore, then came back. It just seems like a nice, quiet, cozy, homey hostel in the Hebrides.

<> <> <> <> <>

October 5
Berneray

I slept so deeply that by the time I got up, everyone but Doug had departed on their travels. After leisurely tea, yogurt, bread and jam, and a visit from Jessie and her dog Roy, who didn't like you to stop petting him once you started, I decided to venture out in the wind and rain to the nearby tiny post office for postcards, an onion from the nearby store, and to the nearer passenger ferry jetty to pick up the new winter ferry schedule for the hostel.

I found postcards, but no ferry schedule, and an onion and other goodies, including bandaids, from the nice older lady at the store, and many, many friendly folk. I have decided that the measure of a Good Place on these islands is which place has onions. So far they all do!

As I neared the hostel (the rain had almost stopped), a jeep stopped to pick me up (I wasn't thumbing). It was the woman who crossed on the ferry with us yesterday and the people she's staying with. One of the men told me how the sea is slowly eating away the coastline. It used to be that the hostels were further back from the sea. Here we're surrounded by the Sound of Harris, and further southeast, the Little Minch, the southern extension of the Minch. The mythical blue men of the Minch, also known as storm kelpies, inhabit the waters in this area, looking for sailors to drown and stricken boats to sink, or so the fables go. The people dropped me off right at the hostel.

I ate lunch, and as the weather slacked off again, Doug decided to stir from reading his book and go out for a walk. I had the brilliant idea, while everyone was gone, to take a hot scoop bath, as the water from the sink in the common room is scalding hot. Why didn't I think of that before? I used a big cooking pot, filled it with steaming water, took it to the bathroom with a coffee cup, and pretended it was a hot shower. I felt so clean afterwards!

I was so sure the sun would appear – it always has – but when Doug got back, it was blowing in earnest, with no sign of letting up or the wall of rain clouds breaking. So I sat down to read my *Mists of Avalon* and write all day, as the ocean wind howled over the little isle of Berneray. It was easy just to sit inside out of the weather - like the locals did. It was easy to picture myself staying here for a week, like many of these hostelers have done!

After a while I ventured bravely out into the wind, along the sandy shore where it appeared the tide was going out. But I wore my contact lenses, and when I figured out all that stuff hitting me wasn't just little raindrops, it was blowing sand, I knew my eyes wouldn't last long.

So I returned to the cozy insides of the hostel and had another cup of tea, to, you know, contemplate things. Time slows down here. There's no need to rush to do this or that, and if you don't get around to doing something, well, it just wasn't that important.

But eventually I was itching to get out more, so I put my glasses on and I bundled up – rain pants over jeans, raincoat over jacket over sweatshirt over T-shirt, wool mittens; and with my camera I journeyed out into the gale. After all, I am here to experience the Outer Hebrides, and the weather is an inextricable part of it. The wind must have been 45 miles an hour again, right in my face; I couldn't hear the waves for the roaring of the wind in and around my hood, even with it cinched down tight.

Shells littered the ground everywhere; there's a collection of treasures at the hostel that people pick up and leave there, including shells, feathers, sheep skulls and horns, pottery, glass, unidentifiable objects.

The sea was oh-so-rough, different streaks of bright and dark green, gray topped with white caps. I followed the white sand bar around the 'Bay of Skulls,' Doug calls it (because you find sheep skulls washed up there), finding no skulls but a big round lump of stranded jellyfish and ropes, being buried by sand. The wind and waves eat away the shoreline and the sand buries just about anything that washes up if it can't move fast enough.

I came to a rockier shore on the northwest side of the island and crawled along on them because of low tide. It looked for sure that the rain on Isle of Harris to the northeast would charge over the sound and soak me, but even if the cloud did make it over, I think the wind was blowing too hard for the raindrops to land.

Not too long before I reached the dunes, I decided to hike up the hill I was circling, known as Beinn Shlèibhe (Moor Hill), at 305 feet. It was the easiest uphill hike I ever did with the gale at my back. On top I took pictures and stood facing into the wind, marveling at the force – at least 55 miles an hour - and how, literally, I could lean into it at a 45-degree angle. I felt I could have run and jumped with it and flown. The seagulls have to really work to earn their salt here if they are trying to fly anywhere into the wind.

I headed back down the side of the hill around a herd of sheep, grazing as if a hurricane was the norm, aiming for where I thought I had seen a standing stone from below. It turned out to be a standing pole or tree trunk (not a living tree), and above it I was sure I found some real standing stones, in what may or may not have resembled a circle. Were they old or new? They weren't marked on the map I had.

The wind at my back buffeted me speedily toward the hostel. I saw Annie and Jessie and Roy across the way and I waved to them. A white car drove up to the hostel: the smooching German couple from Howmore had arrived.

Doug was still inside. He hadn't ventured out other than to the post office around noon. After being here for 10 days now, he'd done all the wandering in the thrilling wind that he wanted, but he felt no need to move on again yet.

As I started cooking dinner, Jessie, or was it Annie, came in to check on guests. Doug says he can't quite tell them apart either, but Annie's shy and usually doesn't like to talk to people, so this must have been Jessie.

And with dark coming and the wind still howling a gale outside, in blows another guy through the front door, and I heard from his first few words he was American. It was Tom from Boston. He said the short ferry ride was quite entertaining!

This was the fun of hostelling: together we random travelers cooked, ate, talked, wrote; the Germans sat by the stove, Andrea reading quietly to Olaf. Doug suggested a game of cards, and we pulled out a card deck and called the Germans over, and Doug taught us all to play Danish Bastard.

It was quite fun, and then Olaf fetched his rum from his car and we sipped at that, and the game got even more fun.

We were just sitting down to play our last hand before bed when I saw the headlights of a car drive up. The wind was still howling a symphony, rattling the windows and singing harmonic tunes through the thatched roof, it was pitch dark outside, and we wondered who the heck that would be at this time of night.

We heard the outer door jiggle, then a tap on the windows. We all jumped and looked at each other with big eyes. It was a bit...well, spooky.

In burst Norman MacAskill. I spent all night and next morning trying to come up with one word to describe Norman. Doug came up with it: sozzled. I don't know what it means, but I am sure it defines Norman.

He was 48, drunk out of his mind, eyes bloodshot red, carrying (none too gently) a bag of eggs. He gushed in, babbling a mixture of English and Gaelic, "Wood y'be wontin' eny ayggs! Sorry SAR! W'd YOO be wontin' eny ayggs SAR! 'M Sorry SAR! Ahm no p'lice d'tective now n' ~~na faoghla beinn tuath a deas n ayggs!"

His eyes flew wildly from one of us to the other and he gestured with his bag of eggs; the five of us sat speechless – not knowing whether to be frightened or laugh or *what*, when Doug had the sense to rescue the bag of eggs and say, "Yes, OK," since everyone else saying, "No, no, don't need any eggs!" had no effect.

After a few more of his staccato bursts he pulled Tom and Olaf outside, and then he burst back in, raving on in heavily accented Gaelic and English.

Olaf said, "Would you like some rum?" I groaned, Oh, God, and Norman plopped happily down in a chair at the table and his face got even more beatific, as he sipped rum and rattled on, like staccato bursts from a machine gun, repeating things over and over, jumping from English to Gaelic without knowing, skipping from subject to subject, asking questions of one person, forgetting to wait for the answer, forgetting he asked, jumping to another subject, stopping mid-sentence, switching to a strange humming and fiddling motion with his fingers, before pausing for breath and bursting forth again.

"Twenty-eight yeers aht SEA! I was a sea captain! TWENTY-EIGHT YEERS! Y' kno the waves ~~calana is Carla bhagh mhor an eilean nobhaighfleoide MacAskill! Seven foot NIEEN! I's a wee leetl' baby! Not like mmmmmmm 50,000 pounds ~~bhaigh tuath deas nanlean – sowrry SAR? 50,000 POUNDS! K'n y' oonderstan' m' Gaelic? Soorry SAR? Seven foot NIEEN ~~fte oghla beinn deafin tuath an aye, hmmm hmmm hmmm hm hmm," ad nauseum, for an hour.

We all still sat gobsmacked, laughing, slipping each other goggle-eyed looks. Norman was very entertaining. I stared at him thinking, this is so unbelievable. Nobody would believe this. Do I believe this? Is this really happening? If only I had a video camera! I didn't have my camera flash attachment handy, and wasn't sure what sort of reaction I might provoke. And anyway, it was kind of personal and endearing, having this possible former sea captain entertaining us with real or imagined stories we did not comprehend. I wish we could have understood some of his sailing adventures.

I did remember reading somewhere about the seven-foot-nine-inch giant, Angus MacAskill from the early to mid-1800s, so I knew sozzled Norman's stories were at least based on *something*; the giant must have been an ancestor. I could certainly see how legends and myths are created and passed on.

At about 11:30 PM Tom propitiously set his wristwatch alarm off – which Norman didn't notice, he was singing yet another Gaelic song – which we all took as a cue to say, "Oh goodness! Look at that! It's bedtime!" and we all stood up, of which Norman took no notice, missing not a beat or a word of his solo.

That rum bottle still sat tall and available on the table, though it was considerably emptier, and I gestured at Olaf – pick up the bottle and hide it!

He didn't understand me, so I whispered to Tom, "Pick up the rum!"

"Oh! Yes!" He sneakily grabbed it and slid it inside his jacket.

"Well, goodnight," I said, slipping out, leaving them to escort Norman on his way, grateful to be sleeping in the other building.

Talk about getting to know the locals!

<> <> <> <> <>

October 6
Berneray

Doug said Norman fell in the ditch, twice, before he got to his land rover last night. Doug backed it up and turned it around for him to prevent Olaf's car from possible destruction, and maybe preventing Norman from driving into the ocean. I guess on the tiny island here you don't really have to worry about drunk drivers. If you live here, you know Norman, and if you see his car, you just get out of his way, and if you're a visitor, you won't be out walking in the middle of the night in a gale anyway.

I had not one but two wild dreams last night. What's causing them? Tom says it's the ocean. I thought it might be the wind.

Doug had thought about leaving this morning, but he thought about it so long he conveniently missed the 8:30 AM ferry and a ride to Lochmaddy at 10:30 AM. I reckon that's how he's ended up staying at this snug hostel so long. It kind of gives you sticky feet and envelopes you in this cozy embrace on this small island in the Outer Hebrides of Scotland in the Atlantic Ocean. Staying here just feels right.

After a long breakfast of tea, one of Norman's eggs, bread and jam, more tea, oatmeal, more tea, more tea and an apple, which stretched past 1 PM, I figured it would be best for me to stay here two more days. Besides, my clothes that I hand-washed probably wouldn't be dry until Friday morning, and it looked like the weather was going to be horrendous all day.

The wind was still blasting a gale, at least 45 miles an hour at 1 PM, and no one had ventured outside but for Tom to the store. I decided I might have to wait until tomorrow to do some hiking around.

Two more travelers arrived, two German boys. Olaf and Andrea stayed in bed all day. While the wind howled away steadily, Tom and Doug took naps. I disappeared into the *Mists of Avalon*, and the ocean continued its cycle with the tide working its way out.

I felt a bit restless – more like guilty – for not going out, but I couldn't make up my mind on doing anything about it, and by then it was well into the afternoon. Olaf and Andrea appeared at 4 PM in the kitchen briefly, then disappeared into their room again. Tom went back to the store (he said he'd cook dinner tonight). I warmed my rice and lentils for a late lunch. I was still drinking tea. I still get the comfort from cupping my hands around a cup of tea like I did in Nepal, where you tried to absorb all its warmth through your hands into the rest of your frozen, fatigued body. I'm not frozen or tired here; it's just comforting, and I think it justifies the sitting around and sipping tea all day.

At 5 PM it hit me, by golly, I'm going outside! I'm here to experience this, and half the day was gone already! All afternoon the sheep wandered past our hostel in the gale, and where the tide had pulled away from the rocks outside our front door, the wind was already working on forming a sand dune to cover some of the rocks. The sand was always laboring at creating new dunes and sculptures.

I bundled up in my wind and rain gear and went out with the two German boys who were also headed out. We walked up the road in the cold wind, not talking much because it was hard to hear. The temperature had to be in the 30s today, and the wind chill much lower.

The boys continued up the road, and I turned right past the store, heading for the western dunes and shore. The windy, lonely walk led me across a grassy moor, with sheep in the distance on the bare rocky hill, a few deserted houses, and groups of swans that I startled into flight, even though I was nowhere near them. Apparently any human out in this weather was batty and not to be trusted.

I followed an old road track, crawled over three smooth wire fences, wound around the top of wind-and-wave-whipped Loch Bhruist, and crested the little hill to the beach, where sand whipped me in the face so hard it stung and I couldn't open my eyes.

The sea was painted light and dark green, big waves rolling up onto the sandy beach. The sea is like this huge living creature always full of life. This wasn't an angry sea, it was a joyous sea, singing its ocean songs to the wind and rain. I doubted any seals would be following me along the shore today, like they had before. I wonder what they do in oceans like this?

I let the wind blow me along a half mile, then I turned back around, into the wind. It was like walking uphill, or with a heavy pack, or like jogging in place, a steady 50 mile an hour wind with stronger gusts. Such power!

I winched my way back against the wind, and once back on the moor, it eased to a much more bearable 40 miles an hour.

It was nearing dark when I got back to the hostel, and Tom already had dinner going on the gas stove. He said the store woman's husband called this a 'minor storm.'

"They get up to 10; this one's a seven."

The two German boys came in soon after; the German

couple Olaf and Andrea ventured out. I had just missed Annie or Jessie. We were down to our last bucket of coal, so we hoped Jessie would have some delivered, to keep the common room nice and toasty.

Tom made Doug and me cream of chicken soup, rice, and chicken, complemented with a bottle of wine. The German couple came back inside, saying they saw the waves glowing.

That inspired Tom, Doug, and me to get up, bundle up, go out and look, but after a half-hearted gazing in the cold damp 'minor storm,' we all said, "Ah, we've seen it before," and we ran back inside.

The weather's supposed to be bad again tomorrow, and nice on Friday. I've decided I should definitely stay another day and leave Friday, head up to Stornoway and Carloway, move on toward the Orkneys, and be there no later than the 15th. I must continue to move northward, to more wind and desolation, if I am to reach Dublin the first week of November. That's my only real deadline.

At 9:30 we were all a little consternated to see taillights outside the window, but when no one jiggled the doorknob or banged on the window, Doug said, "It's probably our coal. Hopefully it's too stormy for Norman tonight."

Someone had indeed delivered us coal without stopping in to say hi, and we were able to keep the fire going. Everyone sort of quietly faded out one by one to bed.

<> <> <> <> <>

October 7
Berneray

The wind was a bit less intimidating this morning when I crawled out of bed around 9 AM. Some places on earth you look outside in the morning and judge the day by if the sun is out. Here you judge the day on what speed the wind is blowing.

After breakfast and a poor cup of instant coffee from the

common cupboard, I ventured outside. The sun was trying so hard to peek out, and the wind was a rather pleasant 35-plus miles an hour. Starting out to be a grand day, 'twas.

I walked down the road, stopping in at the post office to ask when to meet the post bus tomorrow morning on North Uist. It meets the passenger ferry, which arrives at Newton at 9 AM, weather permitting the ferry, of course, although, "It went this morning, so I'm sure it will tomorrow, too," the postal lady told me.

Everybody smiled and waved from their cars as I followed the road on toward the car ferry and up the hill to the standing stone above Loch Borve. An impressive stone it was, about four feet wide and seven feet tall, it stood leaning south-southeast, with the wind. It was probably built standing vertically, but thousands of years of this wind would tilt anything.

I was buffeted down the hill to the shore of Loch Borve, the sand littered with all sizes of colorful shells, the butterfly ones and swirly ones and others, and chips of pottery. This must be the better shell-hunting shores, despite the protected loch. I saw shells on top of the hill, and shells in the middle of moors, nowhere near the water, either a tribute to the wind, or maybe a time long ago before this island rose from the sea.

Heading back, I took the road west towards the souterrain (a probable pre-historic tunnel); I found where it likely was, and I figured that was close enough. Of course any tunnel entrance would now be concealed with sand and a big rock, which I was pretty sure I had found.

Walking back, I met Douglas on the way to the ferry (I said "Maybe see you this evening," if he missed a ferry, intentionally or not, and returned here for another day, or week), and I stopped at the little store, where I met Olaf. I picked up orange juice, potatoes, a carrot, an onion, and a chocolate bar. Me and my onions.

Doug once suggested, "You could call your book, 'In Search of an Onion.' That could be appealing. Or it could be a tear jerker."

Olaf gave me a ride back to the hostel. His steering wheel

is on the left – wrong, or right? - side. I am accepting of the left-handed driving mode of thinking, so now I'm way confused. It's a good thing they don't have roundabouts here.

Tom was out; I cooked my potatoes and onions and carrots for lunch with my spices of chili powder and cumin that I always carry with me. Olaf and Andrea said they'd cook dinner for us at night when Tom got back. Then they went out.

As the wind picked up again, I sat alone in the cozy hostel and read and wrote, until Tom got back from his walk. Time passed, and Jessie stopped by and saw no new faces. We said said we'd be leaving in the morning.

Somehow the whole rest of the day had passed again and it was dark. I ventured out to the beach, low tide, to see if I could see the waves glowing. It wasn't pitch black though I needed my torch to navigate the rocks near the hostel. The wind was still howling and chilly. I couldn't tell if the breaking waves were glowing or if they were just white from the not-yet-darkness.

It was kind of spooky out there by myself tonight. I don't know why – there wasn't a soul around that was human or non-human that would've come to get me, and I forced myself to stand there and figure out why. I kept having to look over my shoulder, though I knew I wouldn't see anyone or anything, and I felt no other presence. I was just *spooked.* Must be the awesome power of the wind, always blowing, always relentless, always roaring through the hood of my jacket, so I could never *hear* anything else. One of my senses rendered useless. Maybe that was it. Or maybe it was the storm kelpies out in the sea watching.

Olaf and Andrea returned at 8 PM and started dinner; we all chipped in with extra food or help, as they cooked up one delicious pot of pasta and cream cheese sauce.

Tom provided dessert: a ring of pineapple for each of us, with strawberry jam in the center, topped by a dot of leftover yogurt (used to make the cheese sauce).

Olaf got the idea to light a candle, then, "No! Wait!" He grabbed a big spoon and his bottle of rum, lit a spoonful on fire, poured it on the pineapple rings, and voila – pineapple flambé in a tiny thatched-roof hostel with Germans and Americans on the Scottish island of Berneray in the Atlantic Ocean!

After stuffing ourselves, we sat around the table and talked, and to my surprise (and delight), found I was the baby of the bunch. All the others were 33! And the other three are also at that sort of crossroads: now what am I going to do in life, and where?

That's one thing I hope to decide on this trip...though I hadn't really gotten around to thinking about it at all yet.

<> <> <> <> <>

October 8
Isle of Harris, Isle of Lewis

I woke up to my alarm, and a lighter wind blowing, at 7 AM. Just like the locals, I was judging things by the weather. I was sure the ferry would be running this morning. Tom was also up because he was catching the same ferry with me.

After a quick breakfast, I headed out of the hostel just before 8 AM to reach the passenger ferry leaving in half an hour. Tom followed a bit after.

Halfway there the ferryman picked me up in his car and took me the rest of the way. I had a sneaking suspicion he had stopped for Tom first, and Tom had said, "No, go pick her up."

Sure enough, when Tom walked up to the jetty where I was waiting, he said, "And you thought chivalry was dead!"

It took the ferrymen a lot of work to warm up, untie, and maneuver the ferry boat (just like a regular fishing vessel) around and out of the protected jetty into the rough water, just for two passengers and the mail. Going across, we blew the starboard engine and so we putted across very slowly.

The mail bus was at Newton landing waiting for the mail, and it dropped off one passenger for the ferry, and took Tom and me aboard. We bumped along the little one lane road toward the airport and stopped at some little town where another little red post bus was waiting for the mail (and us).

That bus carried us through the rain to Lochmaddy where we arrived at 10 AM. We'd be taking the ferry from there to Tarbert on the Isle of Harris.

It didn't leave until for another four hours, so Tom and I left our packs untended in a corner at the terminal, as nobody would bother to steal those heavy things with stinky clothes inside (and these were the days before abandoned packs would trigger alerts). We wandered the small town before stopping in at the pub where we sat and sipped coffees, waiting for noon when they began serving lunch.

Heading back to the ferry terminal, we ran into Doug. The wind and seas were so bad Wednesday and Thursday that some of the ferry runs were cancelled or delayed by five or more hours. I was kind of surprised he didn't go back to Berneray! He was going to join our ferry which, after it stopped at Tarbert, went on to Uig on Skye.

Tom, Doug, and I boarded the ferry when it arrived. This was a larger ferry than the one from Oban, but it too provided lounging seats only in the rear of the boat. I had to satisfy myself with a forward view by going outside, up a deck, and to the bow outdoor observation deck.

The wind was so strong when I came around that front corner it knocked me back, as well as nearly blowing me back down the steps. It was quite conceivable one could be blown or thrown overboard, and as good as I like to think my sea-balance is, I did take caution nearing the railings where it was a three-story fall into the freezing Little Minch.

Riding at the bow was awesome! The wind whipped about me and my jacket so hard I wondered if it might rip the material. Doug joined me out there once but retreated back inside rather quickly. The sea was still wavy enough that the ship often rose and fell noticeably, like a gentle rollercoaster. A couple of times the bow caught a wave just right and splashed all the way up - three stories - to and over me and a couple of army boys also on the bow. I avoided one good spray by ducking and hiding behind the wall.

After 90 minutes we turned into the large protected Loch Tarbert and pulled into the rather pretty dock of Tarbert, on the Isle of Harris.

I hadn't yet decided what I'd do when I got off – either go on to Stornoway, midway up the Isle of Lewis on the east coast, or maybe go on to Garenin, on the west coast, or, if the bus was already gone (the ferry had arrived 15 minutes late), stay in Tarbert. I wasn't bothered either way, because Tarbert seemed kind of quaint.

I saw the bus, 'Stornoway" (it's so *easy* when everything is in English!) waiting, so, Stornoway it was. I said cheers to Doug and Tom, and hopped right on the bus. Loading right behind me was a woman with an American-tinged Scottish accent.

As soon as we started out of Tarbert I was seized with the urge to ask the driver if I could get off after all; the heavy low gray clouds hanging over the little village somehow made it very appealing. After all, I could have a real hot bath here if I stayed at a B & B...

I'm sure the bus driver would have stopped to let me off, but, I needed to push onwards, keep moving toward the Orkney Islands and Shetland Islands, north and further north.

We passed a loch to the west, which *really* looked inviting with the light shining onto the water below the now-black clouds; and as the bus climbed slowly through the mountain range, I became mesmerized, my eyeballs glued to the window.

The woman across from me, originally from Alaska and now living on North Uist the past 10 years, said this looked a lot like the Alaska 'hills' and tundra she grew up on.

I must've sat with my mouth open the whole way through Harris (technically the same land mass as Lewis, but they're worlds apart in terrain), and I kept blurting out loud, "WOW!"

Harris was formed by volcanic gneiss: "its steely-grey, boulderous mountains, splotched with spongy grass and heather," made touchable by the thick gray mist enveloping the upper slopes that looked as if they could shoot upwards forever, is something I couldn't catch on camera if I had tried, but I don't think I'll ever forget. I'd never seen anything like it.

We passed into Lewis at the Isle of Seaforth (I saw the long road to the Rhenigdale Hostel which I didn't want to walk), and my oohs and ahs died down though I still drank in the scenery like a thirsty camel. It was not as rugged and mountainous, but still hilly, colorful and loch-locked (though not as extensively as North Uist, which was stunning in itself for that very reason).

We passed some acres of planted trees, a lot of which had died from a disease – what a waste. I'm sure the incessant wind makes it hard for trees to get past the baby and teenage stages.

The lady also explained how peat was dug up, a process that makes those trenches that scar the landscape, but really seem to grow back (though shaped a bit differently) in many years. What Tom and I wanted to know was, who the heck discovered peat and that it would burn?

We saw lots of sheep that the bus driver didn't slow down for on the one-lane road, but they always seemed to get out of the way. So far I hadn't seen one sheep road kill.

I didn't really want this ride to end, but we got to Stornoway at 5:30. I stopped in the tourist information building where the nice young man gave me a map and bus schedules and directed me to the Stornoway Hostel on Keith Street.

I said hi to three girls in the kitchen, dropped my backpack, and immediately ran for the bathroom and took a hot shower and washed my hair. I felt like a new human being.

Only then I felt like socializing, with Suzanne from Alberta, Canada (who knew Doug and Lawrence from Howmore), Sarah from New Zealand, two Swiss boys, and Danielle from Australia. I used to think I didn't know the difference between New Zealand and Aussie accents, but there is a big difference.

After we ate together in the big common room, I crowded in with the six of them into Danielle's rented car to a ceilidh they had heard about. A ceilidh is a traditional Irish and Scottish get-together with music, singing, and dancing.

We arrived when one guy was singing. It was an informal ceilidh, in a high school auditorium, with a low-tech sound system that wasn't really working anyway, but very good acoustics for the Gaelic singing. Next was a woman on keyboards and a man on accordion who did a fine catchy piece; then the woman sang a Gaelic song solo. It was brilliant. Her fine, strong, piercing voice hauntingly rang and echoed, blending with the harmonics of the building. I could close my eyes and picture her out on a hill under the moon and stars, among standing stones, singing a solo to the sky.

That was followed by a little skit. As soon as it started, Danielle and I looked at each other and cracked up – we didn't understand a word of it as it was all in Gaelic, but it was funny anyway.

Afterwards back in Stornoway we parked at the hostel, and all walked to a pub. I'd wanted a brew all day, so I had my beer at the first pub, and then I was content to go back to the hostel for bed. After all, I'd had a long day, and although the traveling in Scotland is by no means difficult, I have come to the conclusion that it's the number of different transportations you use in a day that wears you out. (Like today: walk, ferry, post bus, post bus, big ferry, bus, walk). I had a dark special ale, which was good enough, and Suzanne told me the differences between the colored ales.

When we finished our drinks we didn't go home. We walked to another pub (I had no drink). And another pub (I had no drink). They wanted to play pool but the table was taken; they piled their quarters to wait for one to open. I sat, mellowed and tired, watching the same scene you can see in American bars: boozing, showing off, one-upping each other. The music was damn loud, too unnecessarily loud, voices were too loud, the Swiss boys were so cool-ly chain smoking their hand rolled cigarettes. Or, maybe I was just tired.

Danielle had offered me a ride next day to Garenin, plus a chance to see the Dun Carloway Broch and Callanish Standing

Stones, so I felt somewhat obligated to be a part of the gang, but at 12:30, I was done in.

"Gotta go sleep, see you guys. Danielle, if you still want to take me tomorrow, just wake me."

I walked back to my hostel by myself at 12:30 AM, the streets still teaming with teenagers. Stornoway is the only major town in the Western Isles, population about 8,100, so what else is there on these barren isles for the kids to do, but hang out in droves outside pubs, waiting for the day they can get in.

<> <> <> <> <>

October 9
Isle of Lewis

Danielle had been gung-ho pre-pubs last night to get up and leave at 6:30 AM, but it was two hours later before we finally departed the hostel.

It was a brilliant sunny morning, not a cloud in the sky, with only gentle puffs of wind. In her car, we headed across Lewis, northwest on the A857 to the coast, and along the Atlantic coast to the Butt of Lewis, the northernmost point on the Hebrides.

We drove along the two-lane, speed limitless roads, more sheep than oncoming cars on the pavement. At the Port of Ness on the east coast, we drove out to the lighthouse on the point. It was *so* stunning. The sun still shone brightly, the sea raged a brilliant blue, massive ocean waves crashed on the cliffs straight down below us. Wow.

We walked near the edge of some cliffs, and Danielle actually laid on her stomach to peer over the edge, facing her fear of falling off a cliff. My stomach was in knots watching her! I'd never thought twice of standing on the edge of any cliff, but I didn't dare here, with the water crashing and churning hundreds of feet below.

I did venture out on one point where it looked like any

moment a piece would slab off, crumble, and collapse into the sea, like a piece off an iceberg. Then I quickly got off, figuring that even if I am so enchanted with the Hebrides, if it is this rock's time to go, I wasn't quite ready to become a piece of the sea with it.

Heading back down the west coast towards Carloway and Garenin, we stopped at the Black House Museum at Arnol, a restored thatched-roof crafters cottage, complete with a room inside for the animals – an indoor barn-in-the-house, and a peat fire in the middle.

Danielle had to pee, so she asked the folks in the house next door if we could use their loo. Nothing timid about this Aussie gal! They were hesitant at first, but must've seen Danielle's eyeballs swimming in yellow, so they said, "Excuse the house," and let us in. The house was indeed quite filthy, but they had a cute daughter. They were very friendly Scottish folk, so kind to let two strangers in to use their bathroom!

Back on the road we passed a huge, bizarre arch by a house, which I read later was an arch formed from the jawbone of a blue whale – can you imagine the size of this whale! It's the largest animal known to have existed. They can be almost 100 feet long and weigh over 200 tons. Commercial whaling started in Scotland around 1750 AD, although whalebones were used for construction and decoration of dwellings during the Bronze Ages, 3300 BCE to 1200 BCE. The now-endangered blue whale numbered 140,000 in 1926 (and possibly 250,000 before whaling), but are estimated to number only between 10,000 and 25,000 now, due to over-hunting, ship-strikes, and pollution over the decades.

We passed Carloway and stopped at the Dun Carloway Broch, an amazingly well-preserved ruin of a 2,000-year-old Iron Age tower. (In Lowland Scots, 'brough' means fort.) The remains are almost 30 feet high, the outer wall sloping inwards, the inner wall rising vertically, with chambers between the walls. Staircases made of stone slabs lead to galleries.

It's amazing, first of all, how the people gathered and

lugged those stone slabs up to this site, then constructed such an impressive tower. It was a pretty unbreachable defense tower where this race of migrating Celts from central Europe (unique to the Scottish highlands and islands) sheltered from enemies or other tribes.

These people led a harsh life on these bare rocky hills, in the ever-present wind and rain, fishing and eking out a living farming 'lazy beds,' where they dug shallow trenches of peat, and piled that and seaweed or kelp on the ridges between, to form rows to plant in.

From there we drove to the Callanish Stones (*Calanais* in Gaelic) – my first standing stone circle. I kept saying, "WOW! WOW!" Danielle kept saying, "WOW! WOW!" even though she'd seen standing stones before.

The impressive site has around 30 stones of Lewisian gneiss (three billion year old rocks beneath the peat) which stand upright in the form of a Celtic cross, with a central stone circle, erected some 5,000 years ago. Imagine how they dug up and drug *those* stones here. The biggest stone in the center weighs around seven tons.

The full significance and purpose isn't yet known; there was a central cairn used as a burial chamber that later farmers dug up, and planted over and between the stones, because they had to eat and survive. They had no time for rocks, standing or not, magical or otherwise. There seems to be a certain astronomical significance where prehistoric people tracked the movement of the moon. Whatever the reason, there's a certain mystical feel to the place even now, thousands of years later. Danielle told me about Stonehenge she'd visited in England, but this predates Stonehenge.

We drove on, passing a couple of small satellite stone circles a mile or so from the Callanish ring; these surely lined up in some way with the points of the Callanish circle.

From there we headed for the remote town of Uig. It was like driving onto a prehistoric planet. It wouldn't have surprised me at all to see dinosaurs walking about, among valleys, lochs of stunning blue in the autumn sun, near barren hills, rocks everywhere. Standing stones and cairns were common.

The road jogged upward to the coast again, and we drove up a hill to an old Scottish ghost town. It looked like abandoned army barracks, on Gallan Head jutting out in the sea. It was rather creepy. We didn't stop. Beyond was the ever-present stunning blue sea, dark and bright and sapphire, crashing into the cliffs far below.

Leaving that strange place, we continued down the road which swung south along the coast. Below us we discovered an immense white beach we wanted to access. After bumbling about on some random roads with no signs, we found our way. The tide was out, leaving ripples etched in the sand, made by the shallow water when the tide was in. Here the water was such a light bright green (I couldn't think of anything I'd ever seen this color) because it was so shallow, which extended far out into this cove. On the horizon it blended into a blue so dark it was almost black. The ocean! What a stunning array of colors it emanates, depending on its mood and the light, or dark, of day.

We drove on above more stunning cliffs (the word stunning is becoming so repetitious but so accurate), having to stop often to take pictures or just gawk. We continued to Brenish, literally, to the end of the road. It could have been the end of the universe, or the end of time. Or the beginning. There's so much land through Lewis that is untouched. No humans. No roads. Only the barrenness, and who knows, probably hundreds of standing stones or cairns, possibly walked on only by the first inhabitants, who were probably "a Mediterranean people, megalithic builders of the late Stone Age or early Bronze Age, who colonized the west of Britain by sea and built Stonehenge and the Callanish Stones in the second millennium BC." It was so mysterious and other-worldly, it would not have been shocking to see stone age people walking about here.

Following these people were probably the Celts from Europe around 500 BC, the unique race who built the stone roundhouse brochs, scattered throughout Scotland. That would be a challenge some day, to hike and camp down the center of Lewis.

We were hoping for a pub for lunch – in reality the nearest pub was most likely back in Stornoway – but we settled for a small grocery store for an apple and a chocolate bar.

We zipped back to Carloway and up to Garenin and the youth hostel, and as we sat by Danielle's parked car and talked and exchanged addresses, a large person in a white car drove up. He, or she, stared, a lot, then backed up and parked beside us.

The person got out. It was a he, big, windblown, someone you couldn't miss. As soon as he spoke, "Do you know where the youth hostel is?" I knew this had to be the American, Steve, that Tom had mentioned.

"You must be Steve," I said. We three talked a bit, standing by our cars, sometimes heavy discussions for a half hour from two Americans and an Aussie, brought together by chance on a remote island in the Atlantic Ocean.

I thanked Danielle for the fabulous tour, and promised to send her pictures, and she drove off to continue her travels. I learned quite a lot from this 22-year-old who seemed very mature and worldly for her young age.

After a short hike around the area with Steve, back in the hostel I warmed up some rice and cooked up a bland batch of lentils, and sat and wrote the rest of the evening. Garenin is another nice, cozy, thatched-roof hostel with a coal stove (we get one bucket of coal a day, not an unlimited supply), a nice kitchen, and two dorm rooms a bit smaller and snugger than Berneray, though here the only windows are through the thatched roof. The only thing missing here is the wind!

<> <> <> <> <>

October 10
Isle of Lewis

That lack of wind here was so strange! I slipped out of the

hostel early, intending to take a quick hike up to the point on the cliffs on the north side of the little loch. It overlooked the little bay where a whale beached itself a month or two ago, I remember Harri and Doug saying, and then the local folks blew it up to get rid of it. Poor whale.

My quick walk – foolishly, without my camera – turned into a long one because the hills here in Scotland are so deceptive. You think the summit's right in front of you, but there are several folds of rocks and mini-valleys and marshy swamps in between.

I hiked up to the two stone cairns on the highest point around, looking down on the water and cliffs and island, kicking myself that I didn't have my camera. I missed a brilliant picture of two sheep that looked like they were hanging off an abyss (they were) high above the ocean.

I didn't stay out there long because I didn't want to see any more good pictures without a camera, and I knew I'd be back. I returned, had breakfast, sat and read awhile.

After lunch I ventured back out, driven, pulled back up to the ocean cliffs, this time with my camera. I correctly chose to put on my rain gear. Making my way back up to the stone cairns, at the highest one I stood there and stared, drinking in the sights and the feeling: on the western horizon, thousands of miles of the Atlantic Ocean. On the eastern horizon, dozens of miles (depending on how and where the gray clouds hung) of the island, layers of further hills growing lighter until they blended into the gray sky. I stood on cliffs several hundred feet above the sea, on top of the planet, with the wind blowing and the ocean crashing below. This was my church service this Sunday morning.

I really wanted to see a whale; one of the two books Tom off-loaded on me said a beluga whale inhabits Loch Roag, the area I'm in. I stared out to sea for a long time, looking for fins or blows. The commonest whales inshore are the minke and the pilot (the latter is sometimes involved in mass strandings), and killer whales also occur. Whales and dolphins are supposedly numerous in the Hebridean seas; and in the northern Minch in the summer, white-beaked dolphins and Risso's dolphins are common. I watched two seals basking on rocks below the cliffs.

I stood up there and took pictures and marveled, and then was drawn to this one loaf of a cliff attached to the others rather precariously, so that the sheep could get on, but that I was sensible enough not to try.

Still, I was drawn to it, to see *down,* to see the waves crashing in the chasm, trying to split the columns of rocks off completely. Peeking down, I did manage to see a tunnel the water dug through the rock. I did test myself, putting myself in slight danger, not one slip away from death but two, feeling that shooting twinge of fear in the pit of my stomach of danger. Normally I have no fear on a cliff, but here, with the wind gusts, the slippery rocks, and the crashing ocean so far down, my fearlessness shrank into sensibility. It wasn't the smartest thing I've ever done, but, I had to do it and I did it, and then I stepped away.

I didn't want to leave my top-of-the-world perch, so I sat for a while longer in the wind, with a brief, good rain shower hurling big stinging drops into my face, then I reluctantly hiked back down.

Back at the hostel I had lunch then lazed around until evening, when it was time for Steve to make the pasta dinner he said he'd share. Carina came in and joined our cooking; old man David came in and made his own, and we all sat down to dinner together.

We're all leaving tomorrow; Steve's giving Carina and me a ride, if we can all fit in his car with our belongings. I'm headed to Stornoway, Carina to Rhenigdale.

We all faded fast, by 9:30. Before I crawled into bed, I stepped outside in the dark of the Isle of Lewis, drank in the sounds of rain falling, night birds chirping their unfamiliar calls, and the ocean crashing with the tide coming in.

<> <> <> <> <>

October 11
Isle of Lewis

We cut it close, leaving the hostel at 8:15. I didn't think I'd make the 9:30 ferry, but it didn't matter since I'd planned to have to stay in Stornoway a night anyway. Steve flew down the road, and it literally came down to the last second.

We got to Stornoway but got caught in a wee little traffic jam at the roundabout. We got near the pier and, even though it really didn't matter if I missed the boat, my heart started pounding because I had about four minutes before the ferry left. We got stuck behind another line of cars... my heart was thumping, and even Carina was into it.

"Go right! GO RIGHT!" she yelled. Steve whipped right, pulled up to the terminal and braked hard. I jumped out, Carina threw me my backpack, and I ran.

I headed for the further-away passenger ramp but the ferry men waved, said, "No!" and pointed to the car ramp where another guy had just run on. Those ferry men saw me and cheered, "This way! Hurry!" (it sounded like "Huddy") and they yelled to the ferry men on the boat, "Wait! One more!" Apparently they are used to late, sprinting ferry-boarders.

So they held the ferry for me and I ran and ran, feeling like Indiana Jones, just getting through the door at the last second before it closed.

THE SCOTTISH ISLES
- THE ORKNEYS

October 13

After a few days on the mainland of Scotland, I paid for my one-way ticket to the Orkney Islands and stepped on the ferry at Scrabster. I was on my way!

The Orkney archipelago, comprised of about 70 islands, of which 20 are inhabited, is about 10 miles north of Great Britain, surrounded by the North Sea. They've been inhabited for at least 8,500 years, and they have some of the oldest Neolithic sites in Europe. Some of these sites comprise another UNESCO World Heritage Site.

Our ferry was headed for the port town of Stromness on the mainland of Orkney, two hours away by sea. We crossed the Pentland Firth, and skimmed along the cliffs of the Isle of Hoy, battered by the North Sea. And I mean battered – we were in some rough waters. I wore the acupressure wrist bands I had bought for six pounds in Inverness; I don't know that they helped, so it was a good thing the ride lasted only two hours. Whew! What a ride! No corkscrewing thankfully, but a greatly exaggerated and slowed-down roller coaster, huge up and down bobs, the bow rising and plunging thirty to forty feet.

I had to do my usual standing-out-on-the-front-of-the-ferry bit so I wouldn't get barfy. I wasn't about to test the efficacy of those wrist bands by sitting inside. Walking into the gale on the wet, pitching deck scared me, and I gripped tightly onto the rails in front and didn't stay long. The huge rises and troughs were like standing on the brink of a roller coaster, before ripping down. Gripping the railing as I walked, I let the wind blow me (scary) around the starboard side, and stood there a while, still getting sprayed on by the bow churning up these huge awesome waves. Then there was this *humongous* splash that doused the whole front of the boat. I guess the ferry men knew what they were doing, running in these rough seas.

I had to go back inside a few times to un-freeze, then I always went back out, not just to prevent seasickness, but because the water and waves were hypnotically fascinating! I've never been an ocean person, but I could understand how it drew people to make a living on it. There were quite a few people out on deck who must have felt the same way as I did. The mighty sound of the bow smashing into a wave and it splashing up three levels high was exhilarating. I'm going to hear that in my sleep for nights to come.

We passed the Old Man of Hoy, a 450-foot red sandstone stack jutting from the sea, 200 feet from the cliffs it was once a part of. It was hard to get any pictures between the sea spray (not great for lenses) and the unsteady bucking of the boat. Getting pitched overboard was not just a fanciful fear.

By the time we rolled into the sheltered Hoy sound, I was pretty sure the wrist bands weren't made for *serious* motion sickness, and I was having second thoughts about the Shetland Islands next week, eight hours crossing the North Sea. What am I, nuts?

We docked at Stromness, a charming little harbor, and I set foot on the Orkney Islands. I stopped at the tourist office for maps and information, then checked into the popular Brown's Hostel.

I deserved a coffee after that wondrous ferry ride, so I found Peedee's Coffee Shop and sat down to sip coffee, and then ate lunch with more coffee. Afterwards I wandered about town during which time it heartily hailed little ice balls. It was a bit brisk outside, and provided a whole new direction of conversation for the Orkney people. They always have new things to talk about because the weather constantly changes.

A promising sunset turned mediocre, and I kept a shrewd eye on the clouds to the north, returning to the hostel just as it started raining again.

I started cooking dinner – it took 20 minutes to get one pot to a boil, and the other one never did. I talked with a German boy and girl, then took a wonderful, long hot shower, then puzzled over where to go next, what to do and when. It's like school homework sometimes, trying to figure out travel plans.

I solved more immediate travel plans by deciding to stay here at least another night. I went out with the Germans to a pub and had an ale. This was my kind of pub night. Drink one pint, go home.

<> <> <> <> <>

October 14

There were not many backpacker travelers around. Maybe the Wilsons were onto something when they were aghast at my plans to visit the outer Scottish islands in the middle of October.

After a breakfast of tea and dry cereal, I tried to psyche myself up, looking at the sun shining down the narrow cobbled Victoria Street, to rent a bike today. I've never been a big bike riding fan - for me biking is always uphill and into the wind - but it was a good way to get around here.

At 9 AM I went to a coffee shop for white coffee to think about it. It started hailing little ice balls. That did nothing to encourage the thought of biking. I drank my latte and stared out the window, as did the young waitress. She had been to college for a year on the mainland, and is back home here for a year, but when she goes back to school, she's not coming back. "I couldn't live here," she said. She's lived here since she was two.

I decided to blow off the biking and instead take the bus to Kirkwall for the day. The bus drove past the Stenness Standing

Stones, a small circle dating from 3100 BC, and further in the distance, the Ring of Brodgar. Those were in biking distance and could wait for another day.

Meanwhile we drove through waves of sun and rain, which continued throughout the day, punctuated with snowflakes. The weather changed constantly, and it was quite chilly, right near freezing all day.

I wandered the main streets of Kirkwall, and strolled through the lovely St. Magnus Cathedral, founded in 1137 AD. The excellence of proportion effectively disguises its smallness. It puts Notre Dame in Paris to shame. The construction wasn't completed for more than three centuries, and the present building exhibits Romanesque, Transitional, and Gothic architecture. Pillars and arches alternate with bands of red and yellow sandstone. (So teaches the *Let's Go* Bible). I took some prize-winning stained glass pictures.

When it started to rain/snow I stopped for a "cheeseburger roll" and "chips" (french fries, with vinegar of course – when in Rome do as the Romans) and coffee.

After strolling some more, I caught the bus back, through the alternating rain and sun. Back in Stromness the clouds were firmly entrenched, looking rather permanent for the day.

And back at the hostel, it was no longer peaceful. Three loud Spanish boys and two more guys had arrived and taken over.

After I cooked and ate dinner, I bundled up to go back out. I wasn't motivated to walk too far, and since it was starting to rain again, I thought, now's a good time for coffee, although, of course, any time is a good time for coffee. I tried another coffee shop where I was convinced by two other patrons, because of the weather, to also have a slice of the delicious chocolate cake. It didn't take too much arm twisting.

The wee little French press of coffee was great, and I didn't realize I had stayed until after closing. The friendly waitress didn't mind.

Back at the hostel I reluctantly sat in the kitchen/common

room. The three Spanish were sitting in there, smoking, playing cards, and blabbering loudly. I can't get over how these people smoke. And talk! The three Spanish sat at one small table, practically shouting in conversation. Can't they speak quietly? Maybe they are all hard of hearing? Don't they know the value of silence? Now I really cherished the peace and quiet I shared with the travelers in the Berneray and Howmore hostels.

One Scottish guy said he's been here for weeks on Orkney and is looking for work. He's not the type of bright-eyed, eager young man yearning for a job in a sparsely populated Scottish island in the middle of the Atlantic Ocean. Why is he here in the boonies? Maybe he was a fugitive. He wasn't interested in any conversation, just in smoking, and pointing out Martina's milk was over-cooked, and the pasta that I'd cooked should be covered and put away.

Another Scottish guy came in asking for tea, then asking for milk, and helping himself to anybody's goodies that were sitting on the tables. Another guy, an Ottawa Canadian, had that "been there, done that, seen that" attitude, expecting me to be impressed. Gosh. I wasn't. Especially when he lit up and shared his smoke clouds with me. I had to take refuge in my and Martina's little bedroom when a few more hostelers arrived and more smoke clouds lit up.

I am excited to be on the Orkney islands, but it's not my favorite Scottish hostel experience so far.

<> <> <> <> <>

October 15

By golly, I was going to bike today! But I woke up to a snowstorm.

But by the time I got dressed, had a cup of tea, and went out in search of a coffee at the same little café, the sun was out. That seems to be the norm now. Sunshine, then every hour or two a cloud passed over, enveloping the area in a dense gray fog, and it dumped little ice balls or big fat snowflakes for 10 minutes, then it was back to bright sunshine.

I told the lady at the hostel desk, "Of course I want a bike today!" I had just picked up a good map of the Orkneys and Shetlands (also sea-sick pills for the ferry Sunday), and I was psyched up to pedal! Damn the storms! I had my rain gear and this was the Orkneys in October!

I grabbed a bike and set off. I was well layered: shirt, sweatshirt, jacket, raincoat (with valuable hood), jeans and leg warmers and rain pants, and most valuable: wool gloves.

A brilliant sun escorted me as I pedaled out of Stromness, toward the stone rings (both UNESCO sites), and I could see the next snow cloud to the north/northeast, from whence they come. They're easy to recognize now. They look like an upside down mushroom cloud, and the wispy parts underneath are the snow. I could even time when it was going to hit, and I scouted about for a cow byre or empty building to shelter in, and voilé, at the perfect time, I spotted a petrol station ahead, with a big roof. Just as I stopped under it, the flurries began.

As the road filled up with little ice balls, I spoke to an Orknian filling up with petrol. He (like so many other Scottish) thought I was a bit daft, taking my holiday now on the isles. He had a neat little wagon he offered me and my bike a ride in, but I said no, I was enjoying my pedaling. Later I was to wish he'd drive by again because I was so done with enjoying my pedaling.

Turning north from the station, between the brackish Loch of Stenness and the fresh Loch of Harray, I pedaled first to the Standing Stones of Stenness, from 3100 BC. They may be the oldest stone site in the British Isles.

Originally consisting of 12 stones in a large ellipse 144 feet in diameter, there are four or five big ones left, with a low stone hearth in the middle. Each standing stone is up to 12 inches thick, and up to 16 feet tall, and angled on top. "Why?" one has to ask. Nobody is absolutely sure, but the stone circles in this part of the world probably had to do with rituals or burials or astronomical observations.

Miraculously, I had the Stenness Stones all to myself and a few sheep. Or maybe it was the norm this off-season time of year. I wandered about the circle, touching the stones, wondering about the people who found and dragged them to this spot and raised them 5,000 years ago. The place also has a quiet, mystical feeling about it.

The Ring of Brodgar was a mile away, but I could tell I wouldn't be able to pedal there before the next ice shower hit. I looked for shelter but didn't find any; when I reached the stones, it was a full-scale iceball storm. But I discovered that riding a bike in an ice storm isn't so bad, after all, except for the fact it stings when it hits you in the face and you can't see much. You don't get wet! Even my bike seat was dry.

Alas, at the Ring of Brodgar I met the three loud Spanish boys (they had walked), but they were not as boisterous, as the weather seemed to have temporarily subdued them.

It has been hard for archaeologists to date this ring, but it's thought to have been erected between 2500 to 2000 BC.

The Spanish boys left, and I wandered, alone again, among the ring of 36 remaining stones (there were originally 60). This circle is 341 feet in diameter and the stones are between seven and 15 feet tall. One had been struck by lightning in 1980 and had shattered off a slab. The entire area is surrounded by neolithic tombs and excavated dwellings. This had been a very important place, between the two lochs, that people had made pilgrimages to.

There's a stone outside the ring known as the Comet Stone. I really like the local legend as told by Britain Express: "The stones were a party of dancing giants who were turned to stone by the first rays of sunlight. The Comet Stone is said to be the giant who fiddled for his fellows until he too was petrified by the sun's rays."

According to legend, this ring was also used for religious purposes, rituals, and astronomical observations, but then again, nobody really knows.

From there I pedaled onward towards Skara Brae, a

Neolithic village (also a UNESCO site), having often to get off and walk the bike, because my pedaling uphill into a 40 mile an hour wind was slower than walking.

A lazy paint draft horse in a field with a cute face watched me pedal by. A big black dog chased me while pedaling, and barked and thought about ripping my hand(s) off the handlebars. He wouldn't listen to his old lady calling him off. I wasn't afraid; I kept thinking, if you must bite, then please sink your teeth into my leg, not my hands. (I wonder why I thought that?) He kept looking to lunge at a hand, and I'd slowly and politely move it while pedaling, then he'd run around to the other side and go for that hand. Fortunately he was completely uninterested in any other part of my body.

Finally after he asserted his canine superiority he left off. That was good because I didn't really plan a budget for dog bites, and I didn't want my expensive rain clothes getting ripped!

Likewise, I wouldn't fly too fast down the ice-balled roads, not because they were slick and I was afraid of wiping out and skinning my hide off my body and leaving it as a souvenir on the pavement – I didn't want to tear my raingear!

I went almost to Skara Brae, then lost interest. I hadn't really planned to go in it anyway. I had thought, in my beginning moments of biking bravura that I'd pedal north from Skara Brae all the way to Brough Head, but no, it turned out that wasn't bravura of any sort and I wasn't interested in another 10 miles or so of head wind, not to mention then pedaling back!

Besides, another ice storm was coming, so I turned around. When it hit, I stopped because it was so marvelous! I just laid my bike down in the middle of the highway and twirled in the storm. The road turned white, the little pebbles bounced off me, bounced into my mouth (hurt my face) and I crunched them. I was the only soul out on this road in an ice storm on the Orkneys! How many other ancient souls have twirled alone on this beautiful ancient land in an ice storm?

After the storm passed, I pedaled on back. I now know truly what the Scottish/Irish blessing/wish, "May the wind be always at your back" means – it surely was born on the outer Scottish isles! I was lucky that often the wind buffeted me from behind, and I zoomed down some long sweeping hills, in the brilliant sun. I hogged the road when no cars were around. Turning back on the road into Stromness, the sun was almost blinding. Coasting down into the town, I felt a victory. I'd done it! Not a whole lot, but I did it!

I made some phone calls to the Shetland Islands trying to find B&Bs that were open, and had no luck. I called the Shetland tourist office, and they said many places were closed. Ferries did not run back and forth every day this time of year between the Orkneys and Shetlands, depending on the weather and the seas. It's feasible I could get stuck there a week or more, with limited places to stay.

So I changed my plans that I'd had for so long. I decided not to take the eight-hour ferry ride to the Shetlands; instead I'd stay here and travel around on Orkney a few more days then head back to the Scottish mainland.

<> <> <> <> <>

October 16

I took the bus to Kirkwall. The driver dropped me off in town and told me which way to walk to the hostel. I dropped my packs off in the hostel and wandered around the town again. Here in Kirkwall it was raining big heavy drops. But I had all my rain gear on so I stayed dry, though I swished when I walked.

After visiting the cathedral again, and one or two shops I hadn't been in, I discovered I was bored. Now that I couldn't feasibly get further out there, to the Shetland Islands, now what? I bumped into the Canadian boy who's still bored-with-it-all. Maybe now I understand him a little bit.

I stood on the pier in the cold wind, but not feeling cold. Here, now, I am being consumed with my restlessness. I thought this trip is why I'm doing it, to satisfy that, but right now it was not helping at all. I get in these restless states when I'm traveling sometimes, and I don't know why. I don't know what I want, or what I'm looking for, or indeed if I am looking for anything. Maybe I just want to get on to Ireland. This state of being just drives me nuts.

Good thing I changed my mind about the Shetland Islands. They still sound enticing, but I'd be way the heck out *there* with this restlessness.

<> <> <> <> <>

October 17

I found a little coffee shop open in town, so I got to indulge in a satisfying morning coffee before I attended church service in the beautiful St. Magnus Cathedral. The choir, sitting at the center of the cross-shaped church was so smooth and soft, the singing seemed to emanate from the walls and floor and the air around me. It was so lovely! The church was Presbyterian; the city council took it over because its upkeep was so expensive, and they plunged big bucks into working on it. I told the pastor I was visiting from the States as I walked out and shook his hand.

Back at the hostel I was expecting quiet, and darned if the loud Spanish boys were there, making lunch and mucho alto conversation. They said they had planned to go to church, but got there too early, and blew it off. I wonder if they would have been hollering at their usual volume during the service!

In the evening the warden came in and we talked a while. Then the know-it-seen-it-done-it-all Canadian boy returned from his Go Orkney tour and he joined us. He asked me which trek I did in Nepal. I said the Annapurna circuit.

"Oh I did that one. In fact, I've done about 10 of them."

Well whooopee! I could never climb up to that pedestal he's put himself on!

I asked the warden about the northern lights, and he told me all about them, which you can see right from the town, since

169

it wasn't bright with street lights, and not necessarily only to the north. Some of the locals call them "Merry dancers." I want to see them, but so far I've had no luck.

<> <> <> <> <>

October 18

It wasn't until about 10 AM I decided to head to Herston to the hostel there. An ad on the board at Brown's Hostel in Stromness had a hand-written note added to it, "This place is great! Recommended! Use it or love it!" And the lady there had said it's a good place, and people are friendly, and though it's a good three miles from the nearest bus, they'd drive you up to catch the bus when you were ready to leave.

The bus to St. Margaret's Hope wasn't until noon, so I stopped in The Coffee Shop for my white coffee.

Outside it was cool and windy, but like yesterday, no rain clouds, mostly just a film of haze above. I've fallen into the local habit of saying not "Hi, how are you?" but "Hello, nice day," or "Hello, bit windy today."

Yesterday walking out of church a woman smiled at me. I smiled, "Hello."

She said, "It's cold today."

"Ah, yes, but no rain today."

Big smile. "Yes!"

I passed a man on the street the other day. I said, "Hello."

He replied, "'Ello. Cold." It's fun to converse in Scottish weather.

For 1.50 pounds the bus drove me and the other six passengers to St. Margaret's Hope on South Ronaldsay, a little island linked to Burra and the Mainland by the Churchill Barriers, four massive causeways built by Italian prisoners to protect the British fleet in Scapa Flow after the 1939 sinking of the Royal Oak by a venturesome German U-Boat. Hard to imagine a war in this friendly, quiet part of the world.

I got off the bus at St. Margaret's Hope, where I asked a lady leaving a grocery store which was the right way to Herston. She said, "Hop in. I'm going that way." So she and her little twin girls took me part of the way and dropped me off, and not five minutes later a car pulled up beside me and a voice said, "Going to the hostel? I'll take you."

It was the owner Sandy's son, Martin. He drove me to a little two-story vine-covered old house that was built in 1823-4. I was of course the only one here, in a little house by a bay, with an old shipwreck outside my front door.

I unloaded my packs then went out for a walk along the bay, past the six or seven houses that make up Herston. It was historically a fishing village, but not much went on here now.

A few seals swam out in the bay; they'd poke their noses up out of the water and look at me a while, the lone tourist in the off-season, then swim on. I followed the water and cliffs all around Herston Head. It got pretty windy when the wind blew up off the water and up the cliffs, and if I went close to the edge I was either careful or I got down onto the ground on all fours, because I was never completely sure just how the wind was going to whip around.

A lump of rock cliff stuck out into the water a ways, and peeking over the edge, I could see it had three tunnels carved into and through it. Was it human carved? Ocean carved? It had no name and wasn't marked on the map, but if this was natural, surely this place must have had some sort of significance to the early peoples here.

Heading back, I cut across a wet (as usual) field to the road. A yellow truck was coming from the hostel towards me: it was Sandy Annal and his cute little grandson William. Sandy had brought me some coal and started a fire for me in the house, and he said he'd come by in the evening.

I chose a bed upstairs, read, then cooked and ate, then went out back to the cliffs for the sunset. It wasn't spectacular, but it was of course windy, and it was often difficult (it has been on all the islands) to take pictures while trying to hold still against the gusts.

Back at the hostel, which I still had all to myself, I read and wrote until 8 PM when Sandy showed up. He's a sweet 86-year-old who loves to talk. He talked for three hours! We discussed horses, farming, war, Orkneys, history, his political days, and hikers who've been here since he started a hostel in 1972.

After he left, I was quite tired and I hit the hay upstairs. It wasn't all that cold outside, but the serenading wind howled, always the wind, singing through the little roof window.

<> <> <> <> <>

October 19

I heard the wind roaring throughout the night. After breakfast I walked down the dirt road to Sandy's farm. I told him I'd meet him there at 10 AM, and then he'd drive me to see a dairy farm.

Well, I dawdled taking pictures, and there was this amazing rainbow that would not go away, and by the time I got to Sandy's house, he was driving off.

I went up to the house anyway, but nobody was there. As I was walking away back down the drive I heard a tractor at the barn and saw Martin waving at me.

I returned and had a look at their cow byre. The cows are so endearing, stinky, and I think they're not so intelligent. The Annals have two bulls, "Pretty tame," said Martin, petting them – on the *other* side of the stanchions – "but don't ever trust a bull." No worries there.

His cute little six-month-old sheep dog greeted me often with his stinky cow-dog paws. He'd run up to the cows – behind the stanchions where he knew he was safe - and bark fiercely at them, then purposefully run back and forth around them, moving silage to different spots with his nose.

After a while I left, before Martin put me to work with a pitchfork. A car passed on the road before I reached it, and the guy backed up to give me a lift to the hostel.

Soon after, Sandy came by the house and picked me up; we stopped by his place to drop some tractor part off, and talked to Martin. He needed bolts for a tractor wheel, so I went with Sandy into Kirkwall to a garage for bolts. On the ride back he gave me a geography and history lesson of the area.

Then I ate lunch with him and Martin, a can of beans with toast and some meat roll. That wouldn't taste good anywhere else, but with these two Orkney Island farmers, it just tasted right.

While waiting on Sandy and Martin to discuss tractor parts, I read an article on Sandy and his other son who more or less owns the island of Swona with its wild cattle.

Sandy went in the house to snooze, and I walked back to the hostel. Outside was quite calm for once, the wind and wetness seeming to have paused for the day, though the clouds were firmly entrenched, so there would be no chance to see Northern lights.

At the hostel I built a fire, made dinner, enjoyed the quiet. Time passed in its leisurely Scottish island fashion. Sandy stopped by at 10 PM, and we talked again until near midnight. I got a history lesson on the origin of his name, and some of his ancestry. The man is an endless ocean of information. He is sharp as a tack.

I felt bad telling him I was leaving in the morning, and even worse when he sounded disappointed and said, "Oh. I'll be sorry to see you go."

He was driving Martin to the ferry in the early morning but I didn't want to leave that early, or else, "I'd drive you to the bus the next day, if you stay..."

The old man loves company, and he doesn't get too much this time of year. I felt bad enough about my decision to leave that I almost wavered... I'd love to stay here awhile but I'm restless again, and I must keep moving.

<> <> <> <> <>

October 20

On a rare occasion, you meet someone who just Makes Your Day. Sandy was one. Graham was another.

I woke up at 7:30 resolved to leave, still feeling reluctant and a bit guilty to leave Sandy, but my restlessness dictated I must move on. Sandy wouldn't even take my five pounds for staying at the hostel last night, because he didn't have two pounds change.

I promised him that I'd write him. I never knew my grandfathers, but if I did, I'm sure they'd be like Sandy.

I almost stayed. But I packed up and started walking down the road at 8:15, in the sunshine.

Two cars passed me near the village, but they didn't stop, as I didn't stick my thumb out. I passed a field of black ponies, framed by a morning rainbow in the background. The littlest one was very curious about the funny looking human with a backpack, so he came up to investigate, then his buddy had to come over to see what was going on. All this took some time, cutting into the time I had left to get to the main road (it was three miles and the bus to Stromness left St. Margaret's Hope at 10 AM), and giving the surrounding clouds a chance to gather recruits and advance.

I set a good walking pace, but before I got to the main road it started raining, earnestly. I pulled out my poncho over my pack, and although I didn't bother to put my rain pants on, I stayed fairly dry but for my sweats.

Rain was pounding steadily when I reached the main road, and then, of course, *no* cars passed me. Four came towards me, but not one single car was going my direction. Well crap, I thought, I wasn't going to make the bus at St. Margaret's Hope, and the next one wasn't until 4 PM. My pack was light enough, so I figured I'd just walk to and through the town and keep trying to hitch to Kirkwall.

At 9:15 I finally saw a car coming behind me. Come on,

pick me up, I thought, sticking my thumb out. The car stopped, I threw my packs in back, and hopped in the front with Graham.

He was married, and had at least one 13-year-old daughter, but he was handsome, charming, and had a great twinkle in his eye. I said I loved Sandy's hostel.

He said, "That place is a dump!"

When I said I was from the States, he took a shot, "Do you like horses at all?" When I said of course, they're my life, he almost stopped the car. He had a four-year-old gelding he was breaking, though he wasn't real sure of how to go about it, and all he needed was a week of somebody who knew what they were doing to get on him.

Well, I almost changed my mind and stayed a few more days. Graham said he saw the horse running across a hill one day, and his mouth fell open and he said, I want him. He didn't want some plodding old pony for his girl. When he heard I had been at the hostel two nights, and I heard he had this horse just needing me, we both groaned at the missed opportunity.

He drove me all the way to Kirkwall, and I thoroughly enjoyed his company. In another place, in another time... but, nah. This was now, on Orkney.

He dropped me off in front of the cathedral where the bus to Stromness was waiting, and as I collected my bags the bus drove off. Graham stuck his head out his window, "Well that was bloody nice of him, wasn't it!"

I laughed, said "Good luck with your horse, don't rush him," and he drove off.

On the next bus to Stromness, the sun returned to brighten up the sky, and I couldn't stop thinking of Graham. I'll never see him again, (probably a good thing, too), and he'll never know that he just made my day.

Back at the quiet hostel in Stromness (no Spanish boys!), I added my two bits on the ad for Herston Hiker's Hostel: "It's a must-visit!"

<> <> <> <> <>

October 21

The ferry bound for Scrabster, on the Scottish mainland, was supposed to leave the Stromness harbor at 8:45 AM, but it sat with its engines revving for 45 minutes while I ordered and finished a coffee.

Finally we left, and sailed out of the bay into the Pentland Firth. I wore my seasick wristbands, believing in the power of them, and prepared for another doozer of a ferry crossing. Yesterday while driving me through the rain, Graham said, "Yea, it's working up to the Big One tomorrow." He was kidding, but despite this morning's sunshine, I was expecting the worst.

But, to my surprise, relief, and enjoyment, the ride was smooth! The wind and waves were at our back, and the ferry did very little nose diving. I stood on the bow most of the way, not because I was ill and needed the fresh air, but because I enjoyed it so much.

I spoke with a Scottish man and his Aussie wife; he said, "If today's crossing is a 1, 10 being the worst, what would you rate your crossing to the Orkneys?"

"Oh, an 8!" I said, "but the locals probably would've called it a 5!"

I did walk to the back of the boat, and took one last look across the Pentland Firth, to say a farewell to the Orkneys, and to the Scottish Isles.

I was so glad I'd visited, and I was so happy to have met some more lovely Scots, but it was time to move on.

CHAPTER 5:
NORTHERN
IRELAND, 1993

"We regret any inconvenience the bombings may have caused you"

When I decided to travel to Great Britain and Ireland, I was vaguely aware of the bombings and the attacks in Northern Ireland. But I didn't really know anything about the rest of it at the time. It was like a quick little glimpse of something from the corner of my eye.

Ambushes. Murders. Disappearances. Robberies. Weapons caching. The Troubles in Northern Ireland had been going on for decades, and they were still going on. It was kind of incomprehensible anyway - was it anti-British Catholics and pro-British Protestants, or was it the other way around? And why? And weren't they all under the umbrella of "Christians"? Was Christ a Catholic or Protestant or Lutheran or what, and who cares anyway?

But none of that soaked in - this was the modern day 1990s for God's sake, and those are first-world countries! Seriously, how could this stuff still be going on?

Something pulled me there regardless, that inexplicable thing that magnetically draws me to a country. Obviously, it was horses that drew me to Ireland. But it was that Inexplicable Thing that drew me to Northern Ireland.

And so, I went to Northern Ireland, and I fell under its spell.

Three days before I left Scotland bound for Belfast, on October 23, an Irish Republican Army bomb on Shankill Road in Belfast killed 10 and injured 57. It didn't scare me at all, I guess because it didn't seem real; it was like something that happened Somewhere Else.

LARNE TO DERRY
TO BELFAST

October 26

The jumping-off point for my Northern Irish travels was the port of Stranraer, Scotland, bound straight across the Irish Sea for Larne, Northern Ireland.

I boarded the 4 PM ferry. My bags went through an Xray machine. A woman took tickets and handed out boarding passes, while a policeman at the door stopped certain people – like the young man in front of me in jeans and leather jacket, close-cut hair and a leather bag – and questioned them. Like a terrorist is going to say, yea, I'm a terrorist, I have a bomb in my bag here, arrest me.

The policeman just waved me on through – I guess I looked enough like the weary backpacker I was, and I was too tired to be bothered to carry bombs in my little backpack, although, if you'd thought about it, I'd be the perfect cover for a terrorist.

The journey across the Irish Sea took two and a half hours, and, lucky me, it was smooth as glass!

It was dark well before we reached the Northern Irish port at Larne; at 6:30 PM I set foot on the soil of Northern Ireland. My foot tingled: I was here! I don't know why this thrilled me so much, but it did.

No buses were waiting at the terminal; in fact no taxis were there either, so I said well, heck, it's only five miles, I have the crude map in my *Lonely Planet* book. I know how to find the

Ballygally Youth Hostel, and I can walk there on foot.

I stopped to ask a ferry policeman which way the A2 was; he was very friendly and wasn't concerned at all when I said I'd walk there, like it was a normal activity for ferry passengers to walk to the nearest town five miles after dark.

"It's four or five miles," he said.

"Aye," I replied in the Irish/Northern Irish way, "I figure I'll get there by 8:30." I met a few people on the sidewalks, all of whom said hi, and didn't give me a second look as a backpacker. I didn't thumb it (even though hitchhiking in Britain and Ireland was common in these days and I'd done it all over the Scottish isles), but after a mile, a car going the opposite direction stopped anyway.

"Where you going?" he asked.

"To the Youth Hostel."

He turned around and gave me a ride – he was another policeman who had seen me either on the ferry or leaving the ferry. Or so he said. He confirmed it was OK and easy to hitch in Northern Ireland, although, what else would he say as I climbed in his car?

He dropped me off right at the door of the Ballygally Youth Hostel, where I checked in for six pounds with the friendly warden Martin. I claimed my hostel bed, nipped out in the town for a bite to eat, then sat up talking with a couple of Aussie girls into the night.

<> <> <> <> <>

October 27

There wasn't much to see in Ballygally; it was the start of my brief tour up to Londonderry in the north of the country, before heading back south to Belfast. It was a typical route backpack travelers took. Warden Martin said I should have an easy time getting a lift to my next youth hostel at Cushendall.

I psyched myself up for my first-ever real Northern Ireland

hitchhike, plopping my big pack and little day pack outside on the edge of the road and timidly sticking my thumb out, kind of half-heartedly. Thumbing a ride went against *every* grain in my female-United-States-conditioned body. I would *never* hitchhike in the USA. Hitching in Scotland was easy and normal. Northern Ireland was normal, but different. There were *terrorists* here.

A few cars passed me before a blue van stopped; I hopped in the cab with Roy and George, who were heading for Cushendall to do some work. They said they drove past me first to see if I was a male or female: "We was just gonna let the guy walk."

It did strike me, when I first peeked into this van before I committed and stepped in, that gee, what if these were a couple of IRA guys with a van full of bombs that they were going to use!

Then I realized that IRA guys wouldn't be picking me up if they had a van full of bombs, and they probably wouldn't have picked me up anyway because they have other priorities.

And, of course, I did think about being a single female in a van with two guys, who could do whatever they wanted, but then so could have the policeman that picked me up from the ferry, if indeed he was a policeman. These two turned out to be a great couple of guys, and we got on talking horses.

We drove through beautiful scenery along the coast. Everything was so *green,* the hills, and sometimes the sea. There was no other way to describe the color except Northern Irish Green. It was hazy and cloudy (but not rain clouds); the Irish Sea was still benign and smooth as glass; there wasn't a breath of wind; and it was a very mild 60 degrees. They dropped me off in the little town of Cushendall, and it was no more than 10 AM.

The youth hostel was not open yet (many closed during the day), so I dumped off my big pack just inside the door. In those days, people didn't steal things, and no person with any ounce of sense would steal my heavy backpack full of smelly clothes. Armed with my camera and rain pants and rain jacket - always the standard uniform in Scotland/Northern Ireland/Ireland, particularly in the fall - I walked back into town.

After stopping at a bakery for a donut and big mug of milk

coffee, I found the town's little tourist office where a wonderful lady talked with me. If only everyone could be as lovely as the Northern Irish I'd met so far.

I signed her guest book (someone else from Seattle stopped by in May), and she gave me directions to Lurigethan Hill. Not exactly a tourist attraction on the maps but a nice place to day-hike.

Picking a field to wander through, I hopped a gate (and noticed a *large* bull in the next field I had planned to go blaring through, so I changed my path to avoid the bull pasture), and picked the steepest way – straight up. Up and up I tromped, stopping more for the awesome view than to catch my breath.

At the top of this little 564-foot hill, an impressive panorama sprawled through the haze of the Ballymon glen, running down to Cushendall. Toward the south was an arresting view of the village of Glenariff on the sea: green, green, Northern Irish Green.

It was just me and sheep up there. One sheep panicked because his buddy ran a circle around me to safety; instead of following his buddy around, he ran toward me at the barbed wire fence between us, because, I don't know, maybe he thought he'd teleport right through the fence and me to take a shortcut to his buddy.

I thought for just a second that this bounding sheep would leap like a proverbial deer and pull it off, but he crashed into the top strand of barb wire, fell backwards after a bounce – just like those WWF wrestlers do off the ropes – and landed on his back. He scrambled right up and ran away, embarrassed or mortified, I could not tell. Sheep appear to be strange creatures. A Scotsman later told me that all sheep want to do is to die.

There were no humans up here; the locals probably did not find Lurigethan Hill worth a hike but this foreigner soaked up the atmosphere of Northern Ireland. I sat and ate my snack food before heading back down, choosing my route away from the house with the snarling dogs, and through these amazing sticker bushes that tried to tear at my clothes. Back on the road into and through town, *everyone* said hi to me, even kids.

I was the only one in the big, lovely, clean, quiet youth hostel until evening, when a couple came in, a girl from Belfast (going to school in Sheffield) and a guy she met in York.

"Are you going to school also?" I asked him, as most British staying in this round of youth hostels were students. He answered me with great disdain, sneering down his nose. "No! I'm a teacher!"

The English can be so cocky, but their absolute heartfelt right to be so is utterly amusing. He turned out to be nice anyway, and the three of us shared dinner.

<> <> <> <> <>

October 28

I was tired but I couldn't sleep. A noisy plastic sheet covered the mattress, and I kept twisting up my covering bed sheet and laying on and sticking to the plastic. Plus it was stuffy in the room that I had to myself and I was hot. The pillow wouldn't scrunch up, either. Ah, the travails of youth hosteling.

After breakfast, and after saying bye to the warden, I headed out and stood on the A2 headed out of town toward the next youth hostel at Whitepark Bay, where the 9:25 AM bus would come. I thumbed and thumbed, trying for a ride while waiting, no longer timid but rather forceful, which also didn't work.

I got no ride so I flagged down the bus when it came by. Sheep and cattle added polka-dotted colors to the green fields that flew by the window.

Alighting in Ballycastle, I stopped for a coffee and pastry treat in a café before starting the walk out of town to hitch to the youth hostel, which was six miles down the road.

An old man in a truck passed me, then backed up to pick me up; he was a farmer and gave me a lift a few miles, where he turned off to his farm. I stuck out my thumb again, and pretty soon a lady passed me, then backed up to pick me up. She worked in a bank and was on her way to the Giant's Causeway to meet someone, so she dropped me off at Whitepark Bay.

Checking in at the youth hostel with the warden, a young red-haired Northern Irishman with a white little kitty who wouldn't leave his shoulder, I left my big pack and said I was headed to the Giant's Causeway.

"Just follow the water to the Causeway," he said. "It's seven or eight miles." With my light day pack, that was just a couple hours of easy walking.

The beach was white and sandy until I reached low-tide rocks I had to clamber over. Along a climbing cow trail and past a barbwire fence, I hit the real cliff trail, which is part of the National Trust, a British organization that promotes the preservation of natural and architectural wonders. It ran along the top of the cliffs, along some lovely scenery and a turquoise blue calm Atlantic Ocean.

From here I could see to the northeast the Mull of Kintyre of Scotland, and, nearing the Causeway, to the west, Ireland's Inishowen Peninsula.

The ruins of Dunsverick Castle that I passed on the way were decidedly unspectacular and surrounded by scaffolding, perhaps in an attempt to re-spectacularize it, but I have seen so much scaffolding over ancient buildings that I think it's a permanent addition.

It took me three hours to reach the Giant's Causeway, and I was high on top of the cliffs and looking down when I realized I was looking right at it below me. I thought – what? That's it? This is a World Heritage Site? The fourth greatest natural wonder in the United Kingdom?! How blah can one get! Oh well, at least the walk here was worth it for the scenery.

I stopped first at the visitor's center on top, then, since I was here, I hiked on down the cliff trail to the Causeway not expecting much. But when I got there, down to the actual causeway itself, I was gobsmacked. It was incredible! 40,000 mostly-hexagonal columns of basalt formed a honeycomb path from the foot of the cliffs into the sea.

Scientists can explain the phenomenon as a geological freak, the result of volcanic action, but I like the Irish legend better: Finn McCool, a warrior giant, built a highway across the water to Scotland, "for motives of love or war," but he tore it down and this is all that's left.

According to TheGiantsCausewayTour.com, long ago, the giant Finn McCool lived in Northern Ireland. Another giant, Benandonner, living in Scotland, threatened Ireland, and McCool tore off rocks from the cliffs and threw them into the sea, creating a path - the Giant's Causeway - so McCool could reach Benandonner and take care of him.

But it turned out to be a bad idea, as Benandonner was the bigger giant, and he crossed the Giant's Causeway to hunt McCool. McCool hid in Ireland where his wife disguised him as a baby. Benandonner found the giant baby McCool, thinking, uh oh, if giant McCool is a baby, the his father must be a gigantic giant. Sufficiently scared, Benandonner ran back across the water to Scotland, tearing up as much of the Causeway he could behind him. What we can now see along the cliffs is what is left of the Giant's Causeway.

After several hours of climbing about in wonderment, I started hiking back the miles to the hostel on the road. I thumbed and thumbed while walking, almost all the way to the hostel. I quit thumbing two or three miles away because I was so close and I wasn't having any luck anyway. Fourteen miles was good exercise for the day. I could feel my thigh muscles protesting when I got back.

And I was *starved*. That workout made me ravenous. From the food I carried in my backpack, I made tomato soup, a ton of rice, and the last of my lentils. I'm now out of food – nothing to cook and not even any porridge left, and no nearby store.

With no commitments, I decided to go to Derry (Londonderry, which everybody in the know called Derry) in the morning. A youth hostel was open there.

I crawled into bed around 10 PM with the open window by

my head gently blowing a cool sea breeze on my face and the sound of the surf in my ears.

<> <> <> <> <>

October 29

Since I was out of porridge, I paid for a hostel breakfast, two pounds for cereal, toast, eggs on toast, orange juice and coffee, lots of coffee. I certainly get my money's worth in coffee alone.

A tall Philadelphian biker, Ed, with a nice voice, also had breakfast at 8 AM; he told me of a Halloween party in Carnlough, and costumes in the stores everywhere, but it doesn't seem like real Halloween here because I haven't seen any candy corn. And somehow wearing scary costumes in a land where people kill each other somewhat regularly doesn't seem quite right, or sensible.

I wolfed down the rest of my breakfast and rushed up to the road with my packs. I didn't want to miss that first bus, since hitchhiking was dubious yesterday.

I flagged the bus down, and it made its way towards Derry. Many cows and sheep lined the highways. Many school kids rode the buses. They all wore uniforms. Is that just a Catholic thing? Or do the Protestants wear uniforms too? I didn't dare ask the kids.

Stepping off the bus in Derry at 2 PM, I found the hostel right away from a map I drew last night. I checked in for six pounds, dumped my pack, and meandered around town.

The Troubles (the latest ones, anyway) are deemed to have started in Londonderry in 1969. The Bloody Sunday (the Irish rock band U2 sings *Sunday Bloody Sunday* on their 1983 album) happened in January 1972, when British soldiers massacred 26 unarmed Catholic civilians. (The entire conflict would last some 30 years, 'ending' in 1998.)

Now, of course, conflict did not just begin in 1969. It was more like 800 years ago when Pope Adrian IV (not surprisingly, history's only English pope) encouraged King Henry II to conquer Ireland and its "rude and savage people." Britain invaded Ireland. Everything Irish was banned. Irish were killed. Things got worse in the 1500s when Henry VIII proclaimed himself leader of the new English Church of England. Irish Catholics had to convert or forfeit their lands. In the north of Ireland, family lands held for centuries were turned over to British Protestants. The Irish were banished from their farms or became serfs to their new landlords. Wars followed. Slaughters on both sides happened.

The potato blight in 1845, which lasted until 1852, started the Great Famine in Ireland. The British didn't cause the blight but they did contribute to a million Irish dying and a million more emigrating. British landlords evicted their already-starving share-cropping tenants; despite millions of tons of grain grown in Ireland, the British refused to feed the starving and instead exported the grains for profits. It's a wonder any Irish survived, much less a future independent country of Ireland.

Generations of hate, memories of hate, carried forward.

The Irish War of Independence, fought between the army of the Irish Republic (the IRA) and the British Army from 1919-1921 (there was another Bloody Sunday in Dublin in 1920), resulted in Irish independence on December 6, 1921. The British continued their rule in Northern Ireland. Many celebrated. Many seethed. Hatreds simmered.

And on it went, with the current Troubles erupting decades later. You can go down a rabbit hole studying the history. I did not know all of this history when I visited; I still don't know it all. I was just an intrigued visitor, seeing people on both sides as wonderful individuals and the countries on both sides as beautiful.

Every place on earth has been a scene of conflict, every race of people has been involved in conflicts, brutal destruction and peace, utter desolation and beauty. We all carry the genes of our ancestors, of war and peace, hate and love, aggressor and victim.

Much of it from an outsider's point of view is radically different from the people experiencing - or inheriting - the violence of generations.

There were many people about Derry, and busy shops and pubs, no policemen, no guns, and little barbed wire except for strands running over some of the gates on the old city wall. It didn't look like a city troubled with murders and bombs, though, like any city, parts of Derry looked rather sketchy and run-down.

I bought groceries in *the* busiest supermarket I had ever seen. Was this the only supermarket in the north of Northern Ireland? I bought so much food I had to transfer some from my shopping bag into my backpack.

After dumping my food at the hostel, I wanted a Guinness, so by golly, I picked a pub, went in, sat at the bar, and ordered a half-pint of Guinness. It was not a warm beer, but not cold, but just what I wanted.

Back at the hostel, it was after 5 PM and though I wasn't really hungry I cooked dinner in the kitchen that was nice and big, though it only had a few utensils and about three cups. I ate in the TV room, watched news, then watched people watch *the* soap opera, of which I already forgot the name, Something-Street.

I talked with Richard from England and Terry from Australia; and later Maria from Australia joined us. Richard gave me two bus tickets he won't use – a return to Belfast and a return to Dublin.

Terry said he may go to the Hebrides in Scotland, so I dug out my unused Stornoway to/from Ullapool ferry ticket and handed it to him. Richard said to just buy him a beer at a pub.

Was Halloween weekend a good time to go out at night here? Well we did, around 10 PM to a pub that we heard live music coming from and spilling onto the sidewalk.

I bought Richard and me pints of Guinness. I had some random guy take our picture. The music was like an Irish Country-Western flavor.

Richard and I left at 11 and headed back to the hostel, and

Terry and Marie stayed for another beer.

My 12-bed room had just two others in it; I fell into bed and fell right to sleep.

<> <> <> <> <>

October 30

I hadn't decided whether I should take the morning or the afternoon bus, but I woke up with the feeling – get going! One night in Derry was enough. It just wasn't a town that gave off the *come-and-stay-awhile* vibes.

An uneventful 90-minute ride took us past fields of sheep, and cattle, and Northern Irish Green, and we entered the outskirts of Belfast, the capital of Northern Ireland. The first sign of anything amiss was the boarded-up and scaffolded Grand Opera House. One of the Aussies from Ballygally had said, "Oh yea, they bomb it all the time."

Next door the whole lower half of the Europa Hotel was boarded up (also bombed - it came to be known as the world's most bombed hotel, having been attacked 33 times between 1970 and 1994), and the usual road into the bus station was closed and barricaded, so that even the bus driver didn't know how to get in there.

Signs hanging up in the bus station said, "We regret any inconvenience the bombings may have caused you," as if it were just a leaky-roof reconstruction situation, and not the fall-out from shrapnel and bullets and upended lives.

I was slightly skittish walking around on Belfast streets for a while, thinking, that last Belfast bomb went off seven days ago, on a Saturday, right around this time. It could happen again, anywhere. Like in that bakery there. Or in the butcher shop I'm passing right now.

But people were out walking, shopping, driving as usual. I didn't see any police with machine guns, but there were quite a few barricaded streets, in the mainly pedestrian zones, with two cops manning each. But they didn't look oppressed or oppressive.

Looking back, it was silly, but I did get an extreme scare in a café. I was dying for a cup of coffee, so I bravely picked one and walked in, ordered a cup at the counter, and dumped my big pack and day pack on the floor by a table and sat down.

A waitress brought my coffee, and as I sat contentedly sipping, somewhat suspiciously watching passers-by outside on the sidewalk, out of the corner of my eye I noticed someone get up from a nearby table and walk away. And then I noticed the backpack left behind by their chair.

My throat choked up, my heart began ping-ponging around in my chest, because, everybody knows that bombers leave bombs behind in backpacks in crowded places, and ohmigod, what if we are all about to be blown to bits. I felt like sprinting screaming out the door... but I could not move a muscle, so instantly constricted by fear I was.

But this was silly, right? What kind of crazy timing would that be, if I arrived in Belfast, walked in my first café and sat down by a bomber? Surely that could not be possible. But what if it was a bomb and I could save everybody's lives?! *This is how these things happen.*

Just as I was on the verge of saying something, *anything*, to someone, *anyone*, a well-dressed lady walked back and retrieved the pack on her way out the door.

I sure did feel ridiculous with my thoughts, but it took a while for me to calm back down.

And as life continued on the streets of Belfast - people walking by on the sidewalk, people shopping, people coming in and out of the café and sitting to drink coffee, people having conversations, and I did not die by bomb, my heart eventually returned to a normal rhythm, and I was grateful I hadn't panicked and created havoc and embarrassed myself. So this is how life in Belfast is. Either you are scared of being executed or becoming collateral damage, or you are not, and you carry on living.

And so, after walking around for two hours in the city, after I hadn't been blown up, or heard any shots, I ceased to be frightened – more like the Belfastians: Well, if it happens and I'm hit, it was my time to go, though, really, I could not *really* understand what it was like to live here.

I stopped at the tourist office and picked up a city map, and found a flier on an afternoon play, *Twelfth Night*. What auspicious timing! With a theater background, I had to see a Northern Ireland play.

I took a bus to the hostel, checked in into an almost full – and messy – room and dumped my big pack.

Catching a bus back into the city, I alighted near the Old Museum Arts Centre, downed a greasy fast food meal of chicken and chips (before-Great Britain and after-Great Britain cholesterol tests would've been entertaining) and went to the theater, and had a coffee while I waited for the show to begin.

I talked to the lady at the ticket table about my travels, to Scotland, Northern Ireland, and, next, to Ireland: "Go West!" she said. "Go west!" By that I assumed she meant, leave Belfast!

The play was very interesting, by the company Show of Hands, which combines movement, sound, mime, and artistic sign language. The costumes were fabulous.

After the show, one guy from the play, whom I talked to while looking at exhibition photographs on the walls, asked if I wanted to go with them for a brew. "Only place in Northern Ireland you can get an English brew." Oh, well in that case, sure! As if I'd know the difference between an English brew in a Northern Irish pub or not.

Jim was a photographer, and Oona, his wife, is on an Arts Council that supported this play. They brought their six-week-old baby to the pub.

After my pint of some kind of ale I don't remember the name of, two more guys joined us, Jerry an artist, and John the show technician.

I had two or three half pints of Guinness after that, deliberately slowing down my intake. We talked horses and politics. Listening to me talk about my horses, Oona said she has an uncle in Kilmallock, Limerick, who breeds and sells horses. She said to call her later and she'd give me his number.

They left, and I sat with Jerry and Jim (John had to go run the evening show) discussing it all – virginity, drugs (drugs a big thing to these guys – they couldn't believe I'd never smoked pot), gay scene here, the problems in Northern Ireland.

They explained the Troubles to me, but I still don't completely understand it, nor will I attempt to put it to paper. It did come out that Jerry was shot in the back, years ago, (he nearly died), in a drive-by random shooting, because he is Catholic.

An outsider like me would just never know about the problems all these people - both sides - have. The Northern Irish I have met - obviously both Catholics and Protestants - have all been so nice. But I guess that's part of it. The murderers, on both sides, have families they love, and they go to work during the days and they go to church on Sundays, and they do their dirty work at night, and go back home to the families they love. The victims have families they love, they go to work during the days and they go to church on Sundays, and they die and they don't go home. Give me a lineup of Catholics and Protestants and I wouldn't be able to visually see the difference in them. Would they? It just made no sense to me but it ate at me and I couldn't let go of it.

As we had all walked out of the theater heading for the pub, I had pulled up short, startled, as one of those armored vehicles was parked nearby, and several military men with their automatic rifles walking about. Jim and Oona didn't miss a step. "Oh it must be another peace march. It does get a little disconcerting when they look at you through their gun scopes."

But Jerry said nobody really worries, like, oh, another bomb scare, everybody out of the building, ho hum, no rush.

The pub owner sat down with us to chat. Jim and Jerry invited me out to Jim's house in the northern part of Belfast (he doesn't feel safe there, but, well, they live there in a nice place, he said), his wife could cook us dinner and they had an extra room I could stay in.

But I declined, and at 8:30 headed back to City Hall to catch a bus back to the hostel in the dark. There were few people out but I didn't feel any bad vibes at all (of course this wasn't a 'bad' part of town), and I waited at the bus stop for my bus. Quite a few old folks were out strolling, too.

Getting on the bus was a New Zealand guy, Naden, who had only Irish Republic pence and whom the bus driver just let on. At that time of night, armored vehicles drove about the city center, with two men on top, huddled inside with only their shielded heads sticking out, looking down their barrels at night strollers.

When our bus pulled up right beside one, I was right at the business end of a long tank barrel, pointed right at me. My skin prickled, but I just thought, Uh, oh, well, OK then. What do you do but shrug and go about being like the Belfastians.

Our bus drove past the Belfast City Hall, where flowers and signs covered the grass in remembrance of those lost in the bombing a week ago.

The hostel was nice and quiet for a while. I sat in the common room with a Houston girl and the Aussie hostel worker and wrote in my journal.

Then 'the dancers' came in – a huge group of 14 to 20-year-old noisy brats who had left the kitchen in an absolute mess.

They all quieted down when, on the news, a bulletin announced that eight people had just been shot in a pub in Greysteel, 10 miles from Derry.

And it came back to me what Terry had said in the youth hostel Friday night in Derry, before we went out to a pub. He'd said he heard that the UVF or UFF (pro-British Protestant groups), or whoever, was going to take their revenge in a pub on Halloween near Derry – only we weren't concerned because we couldn't decide which day Halloween was.

<> <> <> <> <>

October 31

After sleeping in until 8, and having oatmeal for breakfast in the hostel, I saved the bus fare and walked the hour into Belfast town center. Not many people were out. Sundays seemed to be dead all over the UK.

By then it was around 11, so I thought I'd have lunch, and since nothing else was open, I stopped at Burger King.

I sat at the big window by a street, and slowly creeping up the street toward the Burger King were two military guys, in their flak jackets, helmets, walkie-talkies, some sort of packs on their backs – and fingers on the triggers of their automatic machine guns. They moved slowly, scanning around and behind them, like they were expecting something to happen.

There were six of them all together, with a dog, slowly scouring up the street. One man stopped right in front of me at the window, and stood there, facing the street, a great target for a sniper. I thought – dude! Don't stand there! If someone shoots at you they're going to hit me too!

Slowly they drifted by, some of them ducking behind poles or folds of buildings, just like in the movies. I just couldn't stand it, couldn't believe nobody in Burger King was even reacting to this, so I turned to the family behind me, a mom and pop and little kid, also big targets for bullets, and said, "Um, excuse me, can I ask you something? What are they doing when they do this?"

The lady answered, "Oh it's just a routine sweep." I made such an *oh – haha of course it is!* face, she laughed. They hadn't even noticed it.

After lunch with military and possible snipers on the streets, I walked on into the city center – dead as a doornail. Perhaps all the Catholics and Protestants alike were huddling in their churches.

It looked like a bizarrely deserted city, completely different from the previous days. It even felt different, not menacing but *empty*. Still a few armored trucks drove here and there, and a few police with guns patrolled. A very few people were out walking, but absolutely nothing but the Burger King and McDonald's and a few newspaper sellers were open.

I spent 55 pence for a sensationalizing newspaper about the shooting at the Greysteel pub. It was the *Belfast Telegraph*, seemingly kind of a cross between a real newspaper and the *National Enquirer*.

"Bloody Massacre!" "Gruesome Horror!" it blared. And I fell for it and bought the paper.

I wanted to walk to Shankill Road. I felt a bizarre pull to see it. It was one of the main loyalist (pro-British Protestants) roads in Belfast, somewhat infamous as being the center of loyalist activities during the Troubles. Bombings of Catholic-owned pubs, murders of Catholics, disappearing of Catholics, the Shankill Butchers - all of it so incomprehensible to me, I wanted to see it to try to get an inkling of understanding. I just could not fathom it. I knew it was all real, but I had to see if it looked different or felt different.

But once I left the Belfast city center, and could see where the main road led to the tracks (where it became Shankill Road), there was *nobody*. High rise apartments everywhere, but *not one single person*. It was creepy.

I do not know why but I still felt a terrible pull toward it, but my feet wouldn't go any further. Eight days earlier, a bomb went off just down this road. My heart started thumping. I wanted to go but I could not. I turned around and walked away. I did not belong here. I was neither Catholic nor Protestant, and these were not my Troubles.

I was glad, later, when Bridgett from Houston told me she had walked down Shankill Road on Saturday afternoon, and in her wanderings, was attracted to a building mural of the UVF or UFF, "Then and Now." As she stared up at it, she suddenly realized there was *nobody* out.

Then a little kid appeared at her side, "You're not from here are you?" and he followed her a ways, and she got spooked and realized she probably shouldn't be there. So she turned on her heels and immediately left.

So I walked back towards the Belfast city center, and after passing St. Anne's Cathedral (full for a service), I passed a bus stop where a bus pulled up going to Carrickfergus. On the spur of the moment, I hopped on.

We arrived there around 1:30 and the rather unimpressive looking castle didn't open until 2 PM, and that town was even deader than Belfast.

I wasted time wandering around until the castle opened. Construction on it began in 1178, and the three different parts were built at different times in later centuries. It survived sieges by the Scots, Irish, English, and French, and is supposedly one of the best preserved medieval castles in Ireland/Northern Ireland.

I took my time and looked at and read everything, and petted the nose of the horse statue on which Sir Whatsisname, who originally built the castle, rode, but try as I might to muster enthusiasm, I had to admit: *boring.* Not the coolest castle I'd ever been in – Chateaux Chillon in Montreaux Switzerland still holds that title.

I tried but I couldn't even spend two hours there, so I just walked back to the bus stop. I still had Catholics and Protestants and nice people and inexplicable violence whirling about in my head.

Back in Belfast, as I walked past City Hall, I wanted to head south on Bedford Street, my usual route to the hostel, when I saw a "road closed" sign, with four foot-cops and two motorcycle cops, and four armored vehicles down the street and the patrol men with guns, and an ambulance sitting there waiting. For what, I thought?

So I started to take a detour well out of my way, but I saw other pedestrians (though not many) on the closed street, and by golly, I wanted to go down that street, like the other Belfastians, and not make a big detour.

So I walked back to a well-armed cop, and said, "Is it OK to walk down here?"

"Aye, you can walk wherever you want." He was quite pleasant.

When in Rome, do as the Romans. When in Northern Ireland, ignore the military presence like it's not there, like the Northern Irish do. So I did. I walked past the cops and armed military police, and armored trucks with guys staring down the barrels of their cannons. It didn't unnerve me, it was just surreal. One policeman even nodded to me over the barrel. "Hi, how're ya?"

Three blocks were cordoned off, and by the Ulster Hall and Group theater it looked like some sort of parade or march was going on.

I walked on towards the hostel and bumped into Bridgett from Houston and Carina from Canada. They were also headed for the hostel to meet some other people to then go to see the movie *Hocus Pocus*.

Back at the hostel we gathered Michael and Tamara, the young couple from Minnesota, Ron from New Jersey, and Roger from Australia, and we walked back into the city, to the MGM theaters on Dublin Road.

The movie was silly and hokey, and of course everyone wanted a pub afterwards. After wandering a bit, they decided on the Crown Liquor Saloon, directly across from the bombed Europa Hotel.

We walked into a rather unusual bar that was bright and white and quiet as a church. It was a National Trust Monument, (whatever that was), and had separate "snugs" to sit in in privacy. There was no music at all, which I found refreshing, since music was always too loud and made chatting difficult, though everyone else seemed disappointed.

It crossed my mind that, although supposedly this pub had never been bombed while the buildings around it had been regularly, it was still a well-known bar, and if we were in the wrong place at the wrong time, gunmen could come in here as well as anywhere else.

But that's just how it was in Northern Ireland.

Bomb threats, militia attacks, tornados, flash floods,

earthquakes - you just decide to live with whatever risks you choose to live with, and wherever you choose to live, and you go on with your life as long as it goes on.

<> <> <> <> <>

November 1

It was time for me to head off to Dublin. I was really in search of Irish racehorse activities, and Northern Ireland had been a necessary detour for me. Necessary, because something about the place exerted a peculiar pull over me that I had to answer. The Northern Irish I had met were so nice and 'normal' - I just could not understand how such nice people had such terrible troubles, and why? Why kill each other? It was so complicated.

The more nicer people I met, the more confusing it became, and the more I realized I would never understand.

My attention would be forward and occupied by horses, but always, the whisper of Northern Ireland would follow me, like a shadow: not always in sight, but always there.

EPILOGUE

France, Germany, East Germany, Austria, Switzerland, Nepal, India, Sri Lanka, Thailand, Great Britain, Ireland, Brazil, Russia, Egypt, Turkey, Greece, Italy, Spain, Portugal, Belgium, Slovakia, Norway, Sweden, Denmark, UAE, South Africa, Zimbabwe, Zambia, Namibia, Botswana, Malaysia, Australia, New Zealand, Mexico, Canada, and Iceland, oh Iceland!

There are many more travel stories to share. Stay tuned for that. In the meanwhile, here's a link to some photos from my stories in this book:
https://www.theequestrianvagabond.com/Somewhere-Else-Random-Travels-on-this-Small-Planet

ABOUT THE AUTHOR

Merri Melde, a.k.a. The Equestrian Vagabond, is, or was at some time, and maybe will be again, a horse photographer, writer, photojournalist, illustrator, artist, horse packer, spotted owl hooter, wildlife technician, Raven fanatic, trail builder, carriage driver, sound engineer, theater techie, world traveler, racetrack groom, owner of The Most Beautiful Horse On The Planet Stormy, owner of the somewhat famous Standardbred former racehorse-now-Endurance horse Hillbillie Willie, rabid obsessed endurance rider, and Tevis Cup finisher. But not all at the same time.

Merri has written for over two dozen magazines, and photographed for over three dozen magazines around the world, and traveled in around three dozen countries, sometimes seeking adventure and enlightenment, and often chasing horses.

She's author of:
Soul Deep in Horses: Memoir of an Equestrian Vagabond
Tevis Cup Magic: Taking on the World's Toughest 100 Mile Endurance Ride,
Turn Right at the Sarcophagus: An Egyptian Adventure,
Tales From The West: Four Seasons in the Owyhee Country
And illustrator of
The Alphabet According to Stormy: A Delightful Horse Coloring Book.

Visit www.TheEquestrianVagabond.com to contact Merri and see her published works.

www.ingramcontent.com/pod-product-compliance
Lightning Source LLC
Chambersburg PA
CBHW071022280326
41935CB00011B/1459